Dedication

To my siblings Debra, Charlene and Charles. Thanks to all of you for supporting my development into manhood, education and academia. Debra, you took the responsibility of helping our mother raise your three younger siblings, sacrificing many of the adventures which accompany teenage years. My big brother, Charles, for displaying characteristics of manhood such as bravery, strength and intelligence. And Charlene, for providing the example of spirituality for which many can only dream of understanding.   I am honored to be your little brother.

Foundations of Windows Computers 3.0
Table of Contents
Page I of VIII

Chapter 6
What is an "Application", "Program" or "Software"? .... Page 51

Chapter 7
What is an Operating System?..Page 60

Chapter 1
Introduction to the Book

Introduction to the Book:

There are many concepts in the field of Computer technology. In most developed countries, Computer technology exists in almost every part of our existence. Our cars have systems which interact with cell towers. Our homes have cameras which can be activated by smart phones. We order tickets for events via a website and doctors participate in group surgery between countries via streaming video. Our civilization has truly progressed to a technology-driven society. Due to the 1960's premonitions of what the future would include, I often hear people say, "Where is my flying car?!" When I hear that sentence, I smile to myself for I know the answer to that question. It is not that the flying car has not been created, most people simply can't afford one so companies don't mass produce it.

The People Who Need this Book:

This book is structured in a format to allow motivated individuals to perform many high-order Computer technology tasks. Everyone whom purchases this book may not be interested in certification but simply desire to increase their knowledge in Computer technology. The subjects covered in this text are related to installation and maintenance of specific Computer technology such as Clients, Servers and Remote Access methods. The topics listed in this book are the foundation of every large computer network. Using practical (Or what is referred to as "Hands-On") activities, the readers of this book will master the foundations of Computer technology and be able to perform all required tasks to implement the technology relying only on their accumulated knowledge developed through study, repetition and successful practice. The last chapter of this text entitled "Example Labs and Activities" includes many practice exercises. **The Full Videos can be found on the YouTube Channel "Foundations of Computer and Network Technologies".**

Introduction to the Field of Computer Technology:

For those whom purchased this book to increase their knowledge in order to attain a certification in Computer technology, congratulations! You have the correct book in hand! The tasks which are displayed in the text are directly related to a number of certifications offered by Cisco and Comptia. One of the excellent aspects of understanding one vendor of Computer technology is the ability to "Cross-Learn" other vendor technologies. The term "IP address" is used for servers, routers, printers and cell phones. These "Computer-related device" identities are used on all of the technologies mentioned above. The only difference is "where" you would insert the settings on each platform. This book is created in a "survey-course" fashion and was developed to give the reader the ability to firmly understand Computer-related technologies and to implement them in a production environment ("Real World"). The implementation is based upon "foundation understanding" and utilization of actual technology. Persons presently working full-time in the Computer technology field will benefit from the tasks in this text to learn the technology in order to enhance their organization's ability and functions. Persons who desire to enter the field of Computer Technology will benefit from developing a practical understanding of what is required for Computer-related devices to communicate.

Importance of Earning Computer Certifications:

There are a number of certifications available in the field of Computer technology. It is important that persons interested in the field understand the foundation of what each certification indicates in order to better position themselves in the job market. Many persons outside of the field have heard of different certifications. Certifications themselves do not make a person better at completing job tasks then someone who has no certifications. Certifications do have some essential truths to them which make their attainment highly desirable. It is regarded as true that a person who has certifications will possess the following qualities:

- **Greater knowledge of a specific technology than those without the Certification.**
  - Persons working in the field for many years primarily know tasks and technologies which they have been exposed to via job assignment or troubleshooting situations. The unfortunate association with the learning process is that the person has not been exposed to all of the primary features of a technology. Many features can save organization money as opposed to purchasing many other devices which provide a function that the "on-site" technology already has built into it.
- **Display of letters for hiring entity (i.e., Human Resources, Selection Committee, etc.).**
  - Often times, the group responsible for the hiring process will not understand all the particulars surrounding the qualifications

necessary to fill a technology position. In addition, after learning of all the requirements, it often becomes very expensive to advertise all the desired criteria for a job opening (Often times, job advertising companies charge $1 per word, charged every week the advertisement is available in newspaper or internet format). To compensate for the "word length" of the job advertisement and the review of applications eligible for interview, hiring entities often ask their associates for a better way of advertising a position with the least amount of "words" as possible. This normally results in the hiring entity being told some technology "abbreviations" to use instead of descriptive paragraphs. Take the following scenario for example if the job announcement would cost $1 per month per word:

- ➢ Option A: Human Resources person creates job announcement (Total cost about $51 dollars per month):
  - ❖ The technology department needs a person who can perform the following:
    1. Install Computer Operating Systems.
    2. Install, configure and troubleshoot Hubs.
    3. Install, configure and troubleshoot Switches
    4. Troubleshoot network connections on computers.
    5. Address printer problems.
    6. Answer phones on the Help Desk.
    7. Connect and install Category 5 cable in building.
    8. Connect Computer devices on LAN.
- ➢ Option B: Human Resources person creates job announcement (Total cost about $8 dollars per month):
  - ❖ The technology department needs an A+ Certified technician.
- o Human Resources will now look for applications with the appropriate letters. Other applicants might have years of experience working on computers. Their resumes might also list every item on the job announcement. Human Resources often look at hundreds of resumes per day, however. In fact, some companies have "Optical Character Recognition" (Often called "OCR") software which reads over all the resumes as they arrive via e-mail or posted to a job website. Human Resources attempts

to be as efficient as possible, so they will only respond to those resumes which have the "Certification Letters" they were anticipating.

Examples of International Network Technology Certifications:

There are a number of certifications which are international (Valid all over the world) created by large organizations and professionals in the field of computer technology. Some certifications are "vendor neutral" (Used for multiple companies and technologies) while others are "proprietary" (Offered exclusively by a specific company or organization). In order to gain industry certification, it is often required that a person pass a number of examinations or assessments hosted by the organization which sponsors the specific certification. Your desired area of specialty in computer technology will define which certification might be the most advantageous for you to attain. Some certifications which were active at the time of writing this book are as follows:

- **A+** = This is often known as an "entry-level" certification offered by a worldwide organization known as "CompTIA (Computer Technicians International Association)". The certification displays familiarity with various aspects of computers, printers, operating systems, networks and digital devices including laptops, tablets, desktops and cellular phones. It is also viewed as a "survey" certification because there is no requirement for in-depth or detailed understanding of any of the mentioned technologies. The primary focus of the certification is "Concepts and Knowledge".
- **Net+ (Network+)** = Also offered by CompTIA as a "survey" certification. The primary focus of the certification is also "Concepts and Knowledge". The certification examination assesses multiple terms existing in network technology from the perspective of many different devices from multiple companies. The examination does not focus on any single technology or process from start to finish. This is often viewed as the "entry-level" network technology certification.
- **MTA (Microsoft Technology Associate) or MCP (Microsoft Certified Professional)** = This certification is sponsored by Microsoft and is based on Windows operating systems. Options for MTA at the time of writing this book included Windows 10,

Server 2012, SQL Server, Exchange 2016, etc. Objectives for MTA-related examinations include assessing a person's understanding of network topologies, hardware, protocols, services and the OSI Model

How to Earn a Computer Technology Certification:

There are many certifications which indicate various levels of knowledge in Computer Technology. This text seeks to offer the foundation knowledge which would supplement a program of study for those desiring to achieve some of those Computer technology certifications. At the time of the writing of this book, the following are some of the certifications available in the field of Computer technology:

- **Self-Study and Simulators:**
  - In order to get certified, there are no mandated courses, colleges or training programs. In fact, many certified people have never taken a computer class. Essentially, they were "Self-Taught" after locating resources which would allow them to accumulate the knowledge to pass specific certification examinations. Suggested resources would be the following:
    - **Simulators** = These are a practical tool which allow practicing many high-order tasks required on computer technology. There is no "best" software for each has features which might be advantages for some certifications while not necessary for others. Some simulation software titles would include the following:
      - Packet Tracer (Cisco.com)
      - Virtual Box (Oracle.com)
    - **Certification Textbooks** = These are produced by many different publishers. The book you are presently reading is actually an example of the type used to earn certification. Due to the many authors in computer technology, it would be difficult to say which book is the "best" but there are some methods you can use to select the books which are best for your certification endeavors. The following are a few ideas:

- Talk to technology professionals who have certifications. They can tell you which books and/or simulation software they used to pass the exams.
- As "technology training" programs which books they use. Often time you can purchase the books without taking the classes.
- Certification Organization Websites (i.e., "Comptia.com", "Microsoft.com" and "Cisco.com" often have links to books recommended for certifications. Be sure to check which numbers are associated with each exam prior to purchasing the books. Often books are sold which are associated with "old" and "Outdated" exams which are still using the same name.

- **Computer Technology Training Schools:**
  - Presently, there are many "For-Profit" institutions which have training programs and even degrees advertised as either "Computer Technology Certificates" and even "Computer Technology Degrees". Often times, these schools are called "Career Training Education (CTE)" institutions. These programs possess a broad variety of learning objectives and standards. When selecting a computer technology program, do research on what standards they use to create the program. Questions such as the following would be beneficial when evaluating a potential program:
    - ➤ What colleges or universities will accept the classes and credits from this program?
    - ➤ What is the cost for this program compared to other schools both "For-Profit" and "Not-For-Profit"?
    - ➤ What standards were used to establish the program?
    - ➤ What organizations accredit the program?
    - ➤ Please show me your job placement statistics.
    - ➤ Am I allowed to re-take classes for free after completion of the program to keep skills up to date?

- **Two and Four-Year Colleges and Universities:**
  - Over the last 10 years, many colleges and universities have created "Computer Technology" programs. The advantage to these colleges is that they also confer college degrees which would make a person more marketable in the technology field. In addition, having a degree allows a person to apply for other jobs outside of the field of computer technology if they decided to change careers or needed employment until that perfect "Technology" job becomes available.

There are many institutions available which offer outstanding training experiences. Their costs range from free to extremely expensive, however. Do your research and balance out elements such as your available time and finances. Often times, certificate programs are a good place for basic understanding with the expectation that industry wide certification may follow in the future.

Recommendation on Order to take Certification Examinations:

Although it is not a requirement, having more than one certification is highly advantageous to a computer professional. Multiple certifications will show perspective employers that a technician is an expert in many areas. If a technician had both an A+ and a Net+, they know this person can both create a network and repair all the computers which are attached to the network. Many persons in the computer technology field have a perspective on which examinations should be taken first and the particular order in which they should be attempted. There is no concrete document for most certifications attempts but there are some practical theories on the process. When planning on which certification(s) to take and their correct order, give thought the following:

- What jobs do you have interest? = If a person desires to repair computers and does not want to work on networks there is no need to take the Net+. Simply stick with examinations such as "A+", "MCP", etc.
- Which certification will make later certifications easier to achieve? = Many certifications have similar objectives. Examples of similar test objectives would be such as the following certifications which all have similar questions:
  - A+

- o Net+
- o MCP

Taking the examinations, which have similar subject matter will make future examinations easier. It is like studying once to pass three different tests. There is no definite order of examinations at the lower levels of certification. Simply select the exams that will benefit you the greatest in the smallest amount of time.

Chapter 2
Primary Types of
Workstations and Computers

What is a Workstation or Personal Computer ("PC")?

Traditionally, a "Workstation" is a term for a computer on a network which is primarily used for an employee's access and day-to-day activities. Essentially, a workstation processes activities which do not require permissions from any other device on a network. In fact, a pure workstation normally has only two types of connections such as a connection to the internet and a directly connected printer. The following are some of the tasks often performed on a workstation:

- Checking E-mail
- Writing a document
- Viewing Websites
- Creating a program
- Designing a logo
- Modifying a photo

The above is not an all-inclusive list, but workstations are primarily individual, solo computers which do not require other computers to complete normal functions and day-to-day tasks. Most workstation environments have elements identical to "peer-to-peer" networks, however. When a computer is purchased by an individual in some type of computer store, these would normally be considered a "workstation". This is also the type of system traditionally in a person's home for non-business, mostly pleasure activities.

What is a Client Computer?

A "Client" performs all of the functions of a "Workstation" with a few special modifications. A "Client" requests services, access, or permissions from another computer called a "Server". Essentially, a client computer must ask a "Server" for approval for many of the functions a user might attempt on that client. For example, many clients require a user to input a "username" and "Password" prior to using the client. When the username and password are typed by the user and the "enter" key is pressed, that information is sent to a "Server" for approval. If the Server has knowledge of the username and password combination, a message is sent to the "client" approving the user and then the user's computer will activate. If the user does not exist, or if the user's account is turned off, a "deny" message is sent to the client which prohibits the user's access to the computer. The following are other services a client must request:

- Connection settings for a business network.
- Access to the internet.
- Permission to access printers.
- Permission to access files on computers.
- Access to secured databases.

What is a Server Computer?

In network technology, a "Server" is a system that "Gives out Stuff" or "Approvals". There are many types of servers in operation such as the following:

- DHCP Servers giving network configurations for workstations, phones and laptops.
- Web servers which hold and display websites.
- Video Services which allow access to movies online.
- Email servers for transmitting and receiving texts and documents.
- Security Servers which allow user access via usernames and passwords.
- Domain Name Servers which Domain Name Servers which allow users to find internet websites using a friendly name.

What is a "Thin-Client"?

Some computer systems used computers which have no hard drive and very small amounts of RAM and a very basic processor. These devices are created to essentially access a server in some other location and interact with it. The user cannot tell but all transactions, saves, modifications and tasks are not occurring at the user's location. Think of a Thin Client almost like a monitor and keyboard with an "extremely long" cable which connects it to another computer which can be on another floor of the building or sometimes another state in the country. These types of devices are used at mall kiosks, McDonalds counters for cash registers and doctors' offices for nursing stations.

What is a "Virtual Machine"?

Computer networks include many elements such as workstations, clients and servers which provide many different functions for a company, business or enterprise. Some servers might be responsible for providing videos for companies like "Netflix" while others could be hosting social networking websites like "Twitter", "What's App" and "Facebook". In more secure environments such as banks and school districts, user accounts which allow users to begin their workday, perform automated record keeping as well as transmitting and receiving e-mail are just of a few of the elements supported by workstations, clients and servers. Working with server technology, there is a need to develop experience using many different operating systems and devices which comprise the listed elements. Unfortunately, many of these platforms are extremely expensive. There are options however, which would allow the average person to spend little or almost no money in order to practice and develop skills for administer and managing servers and workstation. This option is often called "Virtualization".

"Virtualization" is the process of using "make pretend" software which can duplicate the functions of real-life computers and servers. Literally, a person can install virtual software on a computer and perform a large number of activities and tasks which would be required on an actual server or workstation. Many of these software platforms are free to the public while others range from very little cost to a price as much as an actual server (Into the "Thousands"). You may ask why some virtualization software is very expensive, well, it is because some virtual software is actually used by major companies as actual operating servers. Yep, a company could literally install 4, 5 or 6 different "Virtual Servers" on a single real piece of steel server. Some companies use this option as a "cost savings" because they only have to purchase one server and they can install as many virtual servers on it as required. These virtual servers are often called "Virtual Machines" or simply "VM's".

Virtual Machines provide support for many of the major functions an actual server performs. Activities such as installing printers, hosting websites, storing shared documents and many other functions. VM's can also interact with the "real world" in activities such as communicating with real computers on a network or allowing access to the internet. There are a number advantages concerning virtual machines:

Virtual Machine Advantages:
- **Quick Duplication and Replacement** = Normally installing different applications and configuring services on an actual server or workstation can literally take weeks. Creating a VM also takes the

same amount of time. After the VM is created, however, it can be copied in a few minutes. This copy (Called a "Clone") can be stored in a safe location such as another computer or a mobile hard drive. The clone is in an "inactive" state which means that it is turned off. If the original VM becomes damaged, it can simply be deleted and the copy activated. Multiple VM clones can be created as needed.

- **Practicing Procedures** = Depending on the options supported by the virtual software, it is possible to make the first VM (Often called the "Master Image") and then make as many clones as needed. After duplication, a technician could practice and perform many activities on one of the clones. Normally, the first few times a technician practices a process, there are a few errors (Or what I like to call "Learning Opportunities"). After a technician discovers the incorrect way to perform a process, he or she can simply delete the operating VM and begin again on a clone. In this manner, a technician can practice as long as they desire until they have perfected the task of which they were interested.   Because they are using virtual machines, there is no damaged to equipment and the use of time is maximized due to not having to reinstall operating systems, applications and other programs.

- **System Interoperation** = VM's can be configured work with one another on a single computer, interact with VM's on other computers or work with actual real computers. Literally, you could create a VM on one computer, create files on it and access those files from a real computer. You could even create a VM on your real computer and perform all of your work required in the real world without changing anything on your real computer.

Virtual Machine Disadvantages:

- **Shared RAM** = Each Virtual Machine behaves as an independent computer. Each VM, like all other computers require RAM. Essentially, the amount of RAM used by a VM is subtracted from the actual RAM on the real computer. Take the following for example:
  - **Real Computer amount of RAM = 16 Gigabytes.**
  - **Virtual Machines amount of RAM = 4 Gigabytes.**
  - **Remaining amount of RAM on actual computer = 12 Gigabytes.**

- **Shared Hard Drive Space** = Virtual Machines require real space on a hard drive for storage of its files and operating systems. The amount of space can be either "fixed" or "Dynamic" (The hard drive size will grow as the VM stores more data). Take the following for example:
    - **Real Computer Hard Drive Size = 6 Terabytes.**
    - **Virtual Computer's Hard Drive Size = 2 Terabytes.**
    - **Remaining hard drive space on actual Computer = 4 Terabytes.**

The major concern with the sharing of RAM, Hard Drive Space and other components (i.e., network interface, central processing unit, etc.) is that it is possible for the Virtual Machine to totally overwhelm and take over all processes from the real computer. When this occurs, the VM's often "Freeze" or "Crash". Even worse, the actual computer the VM's are on may do the same totally eliminating the ability to work on the real computer until the VM's are shut down.

There are dozens of manufactures of virtualization software. There is no "absolute best" virtual software for either practice or actual implementation. Depending on your level of curiosity as well as the amount of money you can spend is the primary determinant of which visualization software. There is no overall "best" virtual software because each has both advantages and disadvantages. I would recommend researching a few in order to locate the platform which would allow the user the options for which ever area of operating systems for which they are interested. There following are some websites which provide access to virtualization platforms at the time of the writing of this publication:

- **Parallels Desktop for Mac** = Runs Windows on Mac's:
    - https://www.parallels.com/landingpage/pd/general/?gclid=EA IaIQobChMI2ejUoKv16QIVlQiICR0HDQb1EAAYASAAEg L54PD_BwE
- **Windows Virtual Desktop** = Virtual Computer software:
    - https://azure.microsoft.com/en-us/services/virtual-desktop/
- **VMware Fusion** = Run various operating systems on MAC:
    - https://www.vmware.com/products/fusion.html
- **Oracle Virtual Box = Software to install server virtually:**
    - https://www.virtualbox.org/wiki/Downloads

- **Microsoft Edge Developer = Pre-Made Virtual Machines:**
  - https://developer.microsoft.com/en-us/microsoft-edge/tools/vms/
- **Microsoft Evaluation Center = Various Server ISO's and VM's:**
  - https://www.microsoft.com/en-us/evalcenter/evaluate-windows-server-2016

Chapter 3
What is Hardware?

What Is Hardware?

In all computer systems, there are two major categories of which all other groups of computer aspects fall within: Computer Hardware versus Computer Software. Hardware is all the parts you can touch, break, throw or trip over. These are the physical devices related to a computer. Examples of hardware could include the computer case, monitor, printer, hard drive, etc. Software is a collection of instructions, files and code which is written out, stored digitally and utilized by a computer to perform operations, tasks and functions. Comparing a person with a computer, the human body would be hardware (i.e., eyes, mouth, hands, etc.) while software would be more like a person spirit (i.e., ideas, morals, ethics, dreams, goals, fantasies, etc.). Many types of hardware can be either Internal (Inside of the computer case), External (Connected to the outside of the case) or Peripheral (Not required for operation of a computer). The following are examples of Internal, External and Peripheral hardware:

- **Internal Hardware:**
  - Motherboard
  - Power Supply
  - Hard Drive
  - Optical Drive (e.g. BD/DVD/CD drive)
- **External Hardware:**
  - Monitor
  - External Hard Drive
- **Peripheral Hardware**
  - Scanners,
  - Microphones,
  - Speakers
  - Mouse
  - Joystick

Hardware Parts in Detail:

This term describes all parts and devices which are attached to the inside of the computers "case" or "box". These devices share the computers power supply. Examples would include the following:

- **Optical Drive** = Often referred to as a "DVD player" which allows access and storage for data such as documents, files, programs, movies, music and the installation of software.

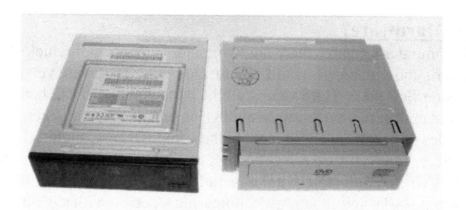

- **Hard drive** = Long term storage for data such as documents, files, programs, movies, music and the installation of software.
- **Motherboard** = Provides the connection for all internal components such as optical drive, hard drive, cpu, etc. All electricity flows thru this component between all devices connected both internally and externally to the computer. This is also the part which is attached to the internal section of the "case" or "box".

- **Expansion Card** = This is a "generic" term used to describe an internal component which can be added to a computer to enhance or add additional functionality to a computer. Examples of expansion cards could be the following:
- **USB card** = Provides additional USB port to increase the total number available on a computer.
- **Network Interface Card** = Allows additional features such as remote desktop or "Wake on LAN (Allows a user to totally control the computer from another location as long as the computer has electricity and is connected to a network)".
- **Sound Card** = Provides for higher quality playback, manipulation or recording of music.

- **Video Card** = Provides the ability to connect a monitor to the computer in order to view processes, activities or videos. These cards can be as simple as allowing a limited number of colors on a display to being comparable to viewing a high-definition television set. Many video cards are enhanced for people who enjoy playing video games. More advanced video cards often have their own processor (Called a **"GPU" or "Graphical Processor Unit**)", RAM and power supply connection.

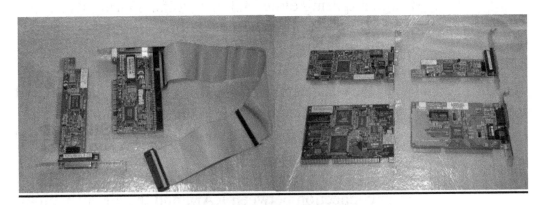

Slots, Ports and Interfaces:

Motherboards and computers in general come in multiple designs which allow a greater range of flexibility concerning the use of the computer. Standard motherboards come with the ability to connect to traditional devices such as a video card, speakers, keyboard and mouse. As time progressed over the last 10 years, other features such as network connections, music and high-definition have now become standard connections. All devices inside and outside of a computer requires a surface allowing connection. The following are some connection methods a technician might encounter. The list below is not all-inclusive of connection types and is meant to simply highlight some of the available options.

The following are some of the connection surfaces available on contemporary motherboards and computers:

- **Expansion Slots:**
  - Interface which allows additional circuit boards (Often called "Expansion Cards") to be added to an existing motherboard to increase the systems functionality. There are many designs such as the following:
    - **PCI (Peripheral Component Interconnect)** = 32-bit design requiring either 3.3 or 5 volts. During its evolution, there are also "subtypes" or "modifications this card underwent during its existence. The following are some of the modifications:
      - **PCI-X (eXtended)** = This upgraded the PCI card from 32-bits to 64-bits. The upgrade allowed a greater throughput of data between the card and the motherboard.
      - **PCIe (Express)** = This allowed more paths for connection between RAM and the circuitry on the card itself. This was a system which was "Backwards Compatible" with older PCI systems. Traditionally, this type of card was used for higher-end, affordable video cards. In addition, many required an additional source of electricity from the power supply using a cable which had a 6-pin connector to link to the actual video card.
    - **AGP (Accelerated Graphics Port)** = One of the original cards used strictly for video and color communications between the monitor and the video card. This was a 32-bit technology and it was designed to communicate more rapidly with the computers RAM. Later versions of this type of card began to include both a Graphics Processing Unit (Called a "GPU") and RAM designed within the card so it would not utilize processing power from the computers CPU and RAM. There are a few modifications for ports of this type such as the following:
      - **VGA (Video Graphics Adaptor)** = This interface allowed the display of 16 colors on a computer screen.

- **SVGA (Super VGA)** = This interface allowed the display of 256 colors on a computer monitor.
  - ➤ **MIDI (Musical Instrument Digital Interface)** = This is a legacy (Somewhat old but still operates) technology which allows a computer to "simulate" sounds produced by real instruments which do not use electricity (i.e., drums, piano, etc.). When recording audio files, they were often very large and required high resource utilizations such as RAM and CPU to process, store and produce the final output in audio format. MIDI technologies used a different compression method which allows almost identical sound quality requiring smaller files and reduce resource utilization. Although MIDI technology still exists, it has been primarily replaced with USB and FireWire technologies.
- **Video Connection Technologies** = Over the last 20 years, video has moved from a few colors to "millions" of colors. To support the increased capability of video, it was necessary to upgrade and design the manner in which video data is transmitted between a computer and a monitor. There are many connection types used for video connections between a computer and a monitor. The following are some methods which existed at the time of the writing of this book:
  - o **Digital Video Interface (DVI)** = This technology allows greater paths for data due to the increased number of "pins" available. Originally, VGA only had about fifteen pins. DVI has 29 pins with and additional longer pin.
  - o **High-Definition Multimedia Interface (HDMI)** = This technology allows enhanced DVI allowing higher data rates on similar video connections.
- **External Ports** = These traditionally enter a "Desktop-Related" system primarily thru the rear of the box. These connections can be almost anywhere on laptop systems. Traditionally, external connections are all "data" and do not supply any electrical power. Most external devices have their own electrical cord which should be connected to available outlets in close proximity to the computer. The following are some examples of "External Connections":

- ○ **USB (Universal Serial Bus)** = USB is the current standard for connecting external devices to computers. USB devices actually have RAM, transistors and drivers on them so there is no need for external drivers, CD's or DVDs. Most USB connection devices are called "Plug-n-Play" and will allow basic standard functions with most Windows Operating System computers such as "Printers", "Keyboards", "Card-Readers", etc. The most popular example of USB technology is what is often referred to as "Flash Drives". USB devices particularly flash drives are differentiated by how fast they can receive and provide data. The following are some of the more well-known data rates:
  - ➢ **USB version 1 = 12 Mbps**
  - ➢ **USB version 2 = 480 Mbps**
  - ➢ **USB version 3 = 640 Mbps**
  When the USB device has many special features, however, additional installations using a DVD or CD are often required.
- ○ **Serial** = This is an almost "all-purpose" port which allows the connection of sometimes older computer devices such as a mouse, keyboard or joystick. This 9-pin-male port is also called a RS-232C or RS-422 interface. Prior to having internet connections in businesses and personal homes, this port was also used for a device called a "Modem" which was used for sending faxes and accessing the internet (Can you say, "America Online Free CD"?). In more recent technology, the serial port is often used to configure high-end network devices called "Routers" and "Switches".

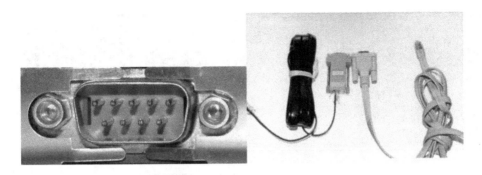

- o **Parallel** = This port uses a 25-pin-female connector (Also called a "Type DB-25") and was traditionally used for older large performance printing and scanning devices. The port is not often on recently produced computers because much of the printing and scanning technology interfaces have adopted USB interfaces. There are still many high-capacity copiers/printers that maintain this interface, however.

- **Power Supply** = As mentioned earlier in this text, this is the component which provides power to all internal devices. The internal devices in a computer require at least three different levels of electricity called "voltage", each of which is supplied by the power supply using different connectors. The following are those rates are listed below with associated devices:
  - o **3.3V (Often just called "3")** = Motherboard, RAM, onboard ports (i.e., USB, NIC, etc.).
  - o **5V** = Hard drive circuits, higher-end RAM and standard graphic cards.
  - o **12V** = Hard drive and optical drive motors, fans and high-end graphic cards

When purchasing a power supply, it is extremely important to consider the number and requirements of each internal device which will exist within the case. Some examples of power supplies appear in the following graphic:

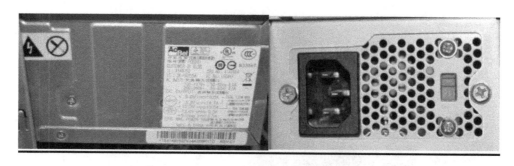

Different power supplies provide different amounts of electricity and must exceed the amount required by the total number of internal devices. The following are some of the traditional ratings associated with specific form-factors:

- **250W (15 Amps) = Micro-Tower**
- **300-350W (25 Amp) = Mini-Tower**
- **400-500W (35 Amp) = Mid-Tower**
- **600-650W (40 Amp) = Full Tower**

If the power requirements of internal components exceed the maximum capability of the power supply, the result will be random computer shutdowns without warning and possible damage to internal devices and/or documents, files and programs. In addition to assuring the power supply will support the internal components, it is important to make sure the type of power connections are physically compatible with the motherboard. The following are some of the Internal Power Connectors which presently exist in computers:

- **Molex Connector** = 4-pin electrical connector used to connect to Hard Drives, Optical Drives and some high-performance Video Cards. It uses a "White" cap with four wires (2 Black, 1 Yellow and 1 Red). In older operating systems, there was also a "Mini-Molex" which was a "smaller" version of a "Molex" which would connect to a computers "Floppy Drive".

- **P1 Connector** = Power connection to the motherboard from the Power supply. There are two designs with either 12 pins or 24 pins (The current standard at the time of the writing of this book)

- **SATA (Serial Advanced Technology Attachment)** = SATA data cables are about 8 millimeters wide with a 7-pin connector holding an associated seven wires. The present maximum length is a little over 3 feet. Another point worth mentioning is that many SATA systems allow the disconnection of a device while a computer is in a running state (Powered on). This feature allows the repair and replacing of failing devices while a computer is currently providing services. This is a great advantage in environments which would suffer if a particular computer was down for any reason. The term which describes this feature is often called "Hot Swappable". More contemporary connections which includes both an "Electrical" type and a "Data" type. Many "Electrical" SATA connection still utilize the "4-wire" Molex for power while others have a smaller strictly SATA version of a power connector. Many SATA "Power" connectors still utilize a "4-wire" standard while others use a "small flat" cable which may be directly connected to a SATA "Data" cable.

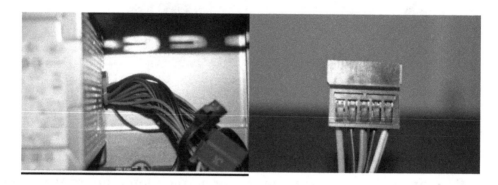

Form Factors

Computers have many sizes depending on the desire of the user or the function the computer must perform. The primary issue which most people view is the design of the "case" or "box" which holds all of the computers "parts". In the field of computer technology, the size of the "case" or "box" not only defines how large the computer is but also other features regarding the computer's capacity to utilize particular internal hardware as well as the ability to expand the computers functions and capabilities. The term used to refer to all the above elements is called a computer "Form Factor". Form factors elements include but are not limited to the following:

- Minimum height and width required for internal components.
- Placement of holes for screws to attach the motherboard.
- Location of external connection ports for printers, mouse, keyboard and network interface.
- Physical size and location of screw holes of the power supply.
- Amount of power available from power supply (If purchased with "case" or "box"). The following are some examples of computer form factors and case types:

- o AT   Size = 12 × 11–13 in
- o ATX   Size = 12 × 9.6 in 305 × 244 mm
- o Mini-ATX   Size = 5.9 × 5.9 in 150 × 150 mm
- o MicroATX   Size = 9.6 × 9.6 in 244 × 244 mm

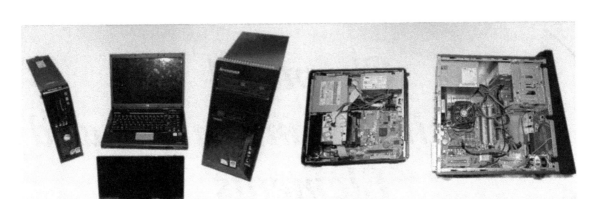

Chapter 4
Processing Components and Elements

Processing Components:

There are multiple parts inside of a computer which actually perform transactions with data resulting in some type of output. The output can be a sound, a document or a light. The following items reflect those components responsible for processes which render some type of output.

- **The CPU (Central Processing Unit)** = The device on a motherboard which performs calculations, manages actions and makes available to a user output resulting from interacting with a computer and associated operating system. In addition to the name "CPU" ("Central Processing Unit", also called a "Processor"). The closest comparison is that the CPU serves a "Brain" for a computer. There are many manufacturers of CPUs for various types of computers such as "Intel" and "AMD". Sizes of CPU's vary but many of them range from the size of a "nail head" to the size of a "thumbnail". Although some CPU's seem larger, the area which is being viewed is actually the ceramic area which surrounds the CPU which provides the dual function of supporting the multiple physical connections between the motherboard CPU port and the CPU as well as a greater area for heat dissipation because CPU's normally produce a high level of heat when in operation. Although a normal by-product of operation, increases in temperatures cause damage to computers, particularly to the CPU. Because it is very important to remove heat from a CPU, they use another device called a "Heat Sink". This is normally a metal object which will lay on the surface of a CPU. The contact of the heat sink absorbs heat from the CPU and disperses the heat into the air. More expensive CPU's actually have fans installed which assists in the disposition of heat. More expensive CPU/Heat Sink combinations also have "liquid-cooling" which incorporates alcohol and other fluids in the heat dissipation process.

- **RAM (Random Access Memory)** = Internal transistor which allows an operating system to store a large number of commands, instructions and results which are accessed by a CPU. The instructions could be in reference to what occurs when icons are clicked, what words are used in a CLI or the position of the mouse pointer on a screen. RAM is also classified as "Volatile" or "Short-term" because when electricity is cut off from RAM, all held instructions are lost. This occurs when the computer is turned off or shuts off because of a power interruption of some type (Pressing the "Reset" button on the case or if someone unplugs the electrical cord on a desktop or even removing a battery on an unplugged laptop).

- **Primary design terms for RAM:**
  - **SIMMS (Single Inline Memory Modules)** = Used on older desktops.
  - **DIMM (Dual Inline Memory Module)** = Standard for contemporary desktops.
  - **SO-DIMM (Small Outline DIMM)** = Standard used on contemporary laptops.
  - **SDRAM (Synchronous RAM)** = Runs at the same speed as the system clock.
  - **DDR (Double-Data Rate)** = Runs twice as fast as SDRAM.

- **ROM (Read-Only Memory)** = The data in ROM cannot be easily modified. This is because the fact that the instruction sets are normally particular to specific transistors and do not regularly require any changes. When a change is recommended, the modification is normally done using special software called "firmware" and requires a process called a "flash update". An example would be tasks a motherboard must perform when a computer is powered on. ROM does not require continual electricity from the power supply on the computer which allows the device to retain instructions for long periods of time without access to electricity of any kind. For this reason, ROM is often called "non-volatile" memory. A very well-known type of ROM is called the "BIOS".

Data Numbers, Storage and Speed:

Depending on the device there are a number of different ways to data can be described, stored, created or transmitted. These different ways to have different terms depending on their utilization or location. The following are some of the terms that you may encounter while working in Computer Technology:

- **Binary Measurement with computers** = In reference to computer technology, most of the essential parts in a computer such as the CPU, video card, RAM and hard drive are described in measurements related to bits in some way. At the time of the writing of this book, the lowest measurement discussed was in the format of "Megabytes" concerning the previously listed devices. After the lowest denomination listed under the combination of "bit combinations" (i.e., Eight "bits" equal a "Byte") the next process of combination represents the subsequent significant measures in computer technology. It is important at this point to define what computer device is being considered however. Depending on the device and its function. The description of the measure will slightly change. Most of the devices in a computer fall into two performance categories:
  - **Item which "stores" bits often use multiples of the number "1000"** such as a Hard Drive, RAM, DVD, and Flashdrives. Examples of this would be the following:

- 1000 Bytes = Kilobyte
- 1000 Kilobytes = Megabyte
- 1000 Megabytes = Gigabyte
- 1000 Gigabytes = Terabyte **(Present Standard)**
- 1000 Terabytes = Petabyte
- 1000 Petabytes = Exabyte
- 1000 Exabytes = Zettabyte
- 1000 Zettabytes = Yottabyte
- 1000 Yottabytes = Brontobyte
- 1000 Brontobytes = Geopbyte

- **Item which "transfer" or "change" often use multiples of the number 1024** such as CPUs, Video Cards, Speakers and Monitors. In addition, these devices often user a measurement term called "Hertz" (Abbreviated as "Hz") instead of "Bits" or "Bytes". For conversational purposes the last "24" is not mentioned, but the measurement is understood to exist. Examples of this would be the following:
  - 1024 Hertz = Kilohert (KH)
  - 1024 Kilohertz = Megahert (MH)
  - 1024 Megahertz = Gigahert (GH **(Present Standard)**)
  - 1024 Gigahertz = TeraHert (TH)

- **BIOS (Basic Input Output System)** = This transistor handles checking each device your motherboard is connected to upon every startup/bootup sequence. Some of the items which are checked would include hard drives, if a video card is operating or if a mouse and/or keyboard is inserted into the appropriate ports. The BIOS transistor is normally attached electronically to the motherboard and is not a FRU "Field Replaceable Unit" (Means it is normally not unplugged from the motherboard). When the BIOS is undertaking this test, it utilizes a process called a POST (Power-On Self-Test).

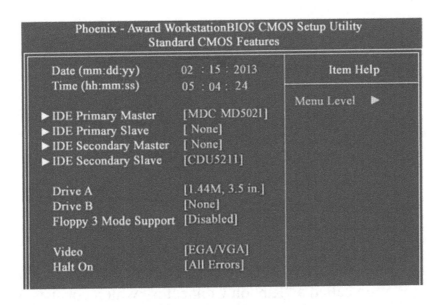

Phoenix - Award WorkstationBIOS CMOS Setup Utility
Standard CMOS Features

		Item Help
Date (mm:dd:yy)	02 : 15 : 2013	
Time (hh:mm:ss)	05 : 04 : 24	
		Menu Level ▶
▶ IDE Primary Master	[MDC MD5021]	
▶ IDE Primary Slave	[None]	
▶ IDE Secondary Master	[None]	
▶ IDE Secondary Slave	[CDU5211]	
Drive A	[1.44M, 3.5 in.]	
Drive B	[None]	
Floppy 3 Mode Support	[Disabled]	
Video	[EGA/VGA]	
Halt On	[All Errors]	

- **Hard Drive** = The "long-term" storage device on most desktops, laptops, servers and other devices (Such as smartphones, cameras, etc.). Anytime a person uses an application such as "Microsoft Word" and access the "Save" option, the first location the operating system will attempt to store the document will be the hard drive. The hard drive has firmware and hardware which allows it to retain data even when no power is being supplied. Hard Drives can often store data for years without any external electricity. Hard drives come in many different styles and configuration. The following are some of the elements involved in defining a type of hard drive:
  - **IDE (Integrated Drive Electronics Interface)** = Closer to the original design of hard drives (Called Parallel ATA) IDE hard drives consist of a metal enclosure which holds a number of metallically coated "platters" supported by a "Spindle". These platters rotate above and below an "accentuated arm" terminating with "Read-Write" heads. The platters have sections which are separated by "magnetic lines" allowing amounts of data to be stored between those lines. Anytime data is stored or retrieved, the platters rotate and the clusters appear under a "Read-Write" head to be processed.

The IDE drive is connected to the motherboard using a cable often called a "Ribbon Connector" which consists of 40 or 80 wires enclosed in a flat cable often gray in color. IDE cables have a maximum length of about 18 inches and maximum data speed of about 133 Megabytes per second. Normally, there is one side which the edge wire is "Red" in color to indicate that side of the cable should parallel the "Red" wire on the Molex power connector. On IDE drive technology, storage and access devices were limited to a maximum of four (Not counting what was called a "floppy disk). The terminators and connections on the ribbon cable uses color standards as in the following:

- **Blue** = Should be connected to motherboard.
- **Gray or Black (Middle)** = Connect to "Slave Drive (Normally DVD/CD or drive with no operating system)."
- **Black (End-Black)** = Connected to "Master Drive (Drive with an operating system installed)."

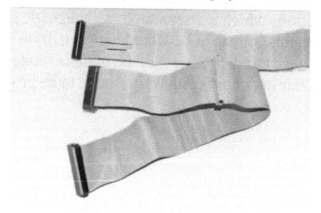

- **Solid State Drive (SSD)** = Although often rectangular in design, that is about the only aspect for SSD drives which is similar to IDE drives. SSD drives have no moving parts but instead store clusters on a type of ROM circuitry. These devices have greater access speeds then IDE drives and do not produce the amount of heat associated with the rotating platters. SSD hard drives are connected to the

motherboard and will support as many directly connected drives as the BIOS is configured to support. Data access speeds for contemporary SSD drives is about 600 Megabytes per second. Solid State do not use IDE cables but instead they use SATA cables.

What is a RAID (Redundant Array of Independent Disks)?

On modern computer systems, oftentimes, the amount of data required for storage actually exceeds the physical storage capability of present-day hard drives. Many companies have emerged over the last ten years with the purpose of data storage services (i.e., Carbonate, GoogleDrive, etc.). In addition, many companies provide services such as word processing, video streaming, etc. These services and storage requirements far exceed the capacity of most hard drives. In addition to storage considerations, the data itself must be preserved and protected against the failure of a hard drive. In order to provide remedy for the prior elements, storage technology has evolved to include a method of combining multiple hard drives for increased amount of storage, faster speed access and drive failure compensation. The resulting process is to connect multiple drives and combine their available space while representing the space as if it were a single drive. The term used for combining the drives is called "RAID". Although literally and physically, there may be 2, or 4 or 32 hard drives within a single computer enclosure, the operating system will regard the drives as a single drive. Depending on the configuration of the system, there are multiple versions of RAID which either stress increase in storage size, storage speed or protection from drive failure. The following are some of the more well-known RAID configurations:

- **RAID 0** = RAID 0 consists of a term called "striping". With this process, equal parts of all data is equally distributed across a number of physical distinct drives. This configuration can be as small as two drives or as large as 32. Regardless of the number of drives, the operating system will report them as a single drive. An advantage to RAID 0 is the speed the data can be written or read to from a disk. The primary disadvantage is that if a single drive were to fail, the entire span of drives will fail.
- **RAID 1** = RAID 1 uses a process called "mirroring" and can be as small as two hard drives. Essentially, data is written to which ever drive is available at that moment. After the data is saved, the other drive then duplicates the data. This configuration is primarily configured to allow the system to continue operation if either drive loses the ability to operate.
- **RAID 5** = RAID 5 consists of striping data across physically distinct hard drives with additional data called "Parity." "Parity" is an "error/failure" correction technology which will allow an array of disks to continue to operate although some of the drives have failed.

No data is lost during a drive failure and the system will still operate normally. Depending on the size of the array (Smallest number is three individual drives.) a large number of drives can fail and the system will still operate. In addition, after the failed drives are replaced with new drives, they are restored by the other drives. After the data rebuild, the new drives will operate as if they have always been part of the RAID.

Hard Drive Elements:

Often time in technology there is a discussion on the design and arrangement of the internal components of a hard drive. Remembering that there are two different type of hard drives in use today (IDE and SATA), there is the need to differentiate the two. SATA drives essentially use ROM technology and allocate blocks of memory for the storage of data. IDE, however utilize a different technology. The following are concepts and designs for IDE hard drives.

- **IDE Drive Components:**
  - **Platter** = This is a metal disc which rotates on a spindle within the drive enclosure. Each platter is coated with a magnetic surface which is designed to hold data. There are normally at least 4 platters designed one on top another. These platters spin at a specific rotational speed to allow data to be either stored or accessed from the platter surfaces.
  - **Track** = On the top and bottom surfaces of each platter there are magnetic "Concentric Rings" which circle the platter. On each platter, the number of tracks are identical and they are perfectly positioned to be above or below other tracks which exist on other platters. Tracks above and below one another are referred to as "Cylinders". The tracks are perpendicularly divided by lines which traverse from the spindle of the platter to the extreme edge of each platter. The points in which the tracks are divided by the lines create specific sections to hold data called "Sectors".
  - **Accentuated Arm** = This armature extends from the chassis and circuit board in the hard drive enclosure to the surface to the "Read-Write" heads. The heads float just above both the bottom and the top of each platter. Each track rotates under or above the "Read-Write" heads allow them to locate related clusters to display data or empty sectors in which to store data within.

- o **Rotation Speeds** = Traditionally, this statement is in reference to non-solid state (Such as "IDE" drives). It is the measure of time required for a single point on the extreme edge of a platter to move in a circle and arrive at its origin position beneath the "Read-Write" head within a hard drive enclosure. The speeds are rated in "Revolutions-Per-Minute" or "rpm". Essentially, the faster the speed, the more rapidly the clusters of data can be accessed for storing and retrieval of data. At the time of the writing of this book, the following were some contemporary speeds of hard drives:
    - ➢ **5400rpm**
    - ➢ **7200rpm**
    - ➢ **10,000rpm**
    - ➢ **12,000rpm**
    - ➢ **52,000rpm**
- o **File Table** = When data is stored on a drive, there must be a manner in which it is arranged. A possible way to describe the arrangement is like a textbook with different subjects. Within the hard drive, there is something similar to a "Table of Contents" called a "File Table" which keeps track of where data is positioned on the drive. When a program is activated using an icon or user typing in a command, this "table of contents (File table)" is used to identify all the clusters related to the program. The platters begin to spin as the read-write heads locate the data. Once all the data has been located, it is loaded into RAM which then allows the program output to be displayed on the screen.
- o **Sector (512 Bytes)** = This is the magnetic device which holds data on a track. A traditional size of sectors in many contemporary hard drives is approximately 512 bytes in size.
- o **Cluster** = This is the term for binary data stored in a sector which has meaning such as a program, document or file. All data stored on a hard drive is broken into multiple sections and stored in sectors. When a file or program is needed all the clusters which are part of the program (Called "Related Clusters") are accessed by an item called the "Read-Write" head.
- • **Arrangement of Data** = When a user performs a "Save" on a computer, the data is written from RAM to sectors on the platters within the hard drive. In order to be as swift as possible in the process, there is no specific order in which the data is stored to

sectors. Essentially, the any non-sequential empty sectors which pass beneath or above any read-write head will receive the data. The clusters are often scattered all over the cylinder as sectors become available. The arrangement of the clusters is called **"Non-Contiguous"** and is the normal method used on IDE hard drives. As the sectors receive the data they become **"related-clusters"** and a reference is stored in the File Table called a **"Pointer"** so the program can be accessed in the future.

- **Drive Fragmentation:** As mentioned earlier in this text, when data is stored to hard drives it is not done in a sequential fashion called **"Non-Contiguous"**. Essentially, the related-clusters are scattered across the platters and cylinders based upon which sectors were available for storage. The pointers are responsible for keeping track of related-clusters to recover the programs or files when requested by the operating system or a user. Often times, after repeated deletion of files, computer malfunctions, reboots, user-errors, damaged sectors, etc., pointers could lose their ability to locate related clusters. In addition, the operating system will periodically check sectors for manufacturing damages (i.e., microscopic cracks, dust particles, etc., on platters) resulting in moving of related clusters to different available sectors on the cylinders. The result of either process could cause pointers to get misdirected from related clusters. The name for this condition is called **"Fragmented"**. A Fragmented drive can result in slow program performance opening documents, slow saving of documents and sometimes system failures. To repair the process when either pointers are damaged or clusters are mis-arranged, the following utilities could be utilized:
  - ○ **DEFRAG** = This utility attempts to move related-clusters closer together and create new pointers to their updated locations. Although the clusters are closer, they are still not sequential or "side-by-side". There will still be "other clusters" or empty sectors between many of the related-clusters which are moved closer together. The term for the condition of the clusters being "closer together" is often defined as **"more contiguous"**.
  - ○ **CHKDSK** = This utility attempts to check existing pointers to ascertain if they are linked to an associated cluster or sector. If any "orphaned" (Not pointing to cluster) pointers are found, the cylinders are checked for the associated cluster and orients the pointer to the correct sector on the cylinder. If a pointer has no

related cluster, the pointer is eliminated reducing the possibility of the pointer causing system slowdowns or errors in the future. This utility can check for errors in both operating system and file pointers. When using CHKDSK, there many modifications which can be utilized. The following are two of the most used:

> **chkdsk /f** = Repairs file system pointers errors.
> **chkdsk /r** = Repairs both file system pointers and problems with damaged sectors (Normally by moving the cluster from the damaged sector to a different undamaged sector).

- **DiskPart** = DiskPart is a utility which allows you to modify various aspects of storage volumes such as hard drives or USB flash drives. It's one of the longest lasting utilities used to manipulate partitions on Windows XP through Server 2016. Not only can it create and delete partitions it can also expand them or decrease their size in real time. In addition, it is a highly utilized to configure USB devices to have the ability to boot-up and access a computer for various reasons such as investigations, repairs are even the installation of an operating system.

Hard Drive Partitions:

This is a term used to refer to areas on a hard drive which are divided by software into sections which reflect a specific amount of space and location. Examples would be the "C:\" drive on a computer. A computer's hard drive can actually be divided into many different sections and display many drives although there is only one actual drive. When a hard drive is partitioned, there are special sections on the hard drive which serve as a "Table of Contents" for the drive. When software is activated or a document icon is "clicked" the hard drive must be able to locate all the sectors on the hard drive in which the document data is stored. The following are some of the methods used on hard drives to keep track of where data is stored:

- **Master Boot Record (MBR)** = This was the method used on older operating systems such as Windows 98, XP and Windows 7. MBR systems have a "size limitation" of no more than 2 terabytes.
- **UEFI (Unified Extensible Firmware Interface)** = This is the current replacement for the BIOS on a number of newer computers. It is the primary standard for systems using Windows 8 and above. It is also

required in the event a computer will hold a hard drive larger than 2 Terabytes.

- **Primary** = This identified which area of a hard drive could be recognized by a computers BIOS. This method was often used when the hard drive was too large for an operating system to utilize. If the hard drive was too large, a "Primary Partition" could be created which reduced the reported size of the drive to the operating system. The reduced section would then be reported as the total drive size. Traditionally, this would cause the primary partition to be displayed in the operating system as "C:\" drive.
- **Extended** = When a primary partition was smaller than the actual drive, the remaining portions of the hard drive could be made available to the operating system and BIOS. At this stage, the remainder of the hard drive is available, but it needs to be configured further in order to be used. In fact, at this stage, the operating system will not display the remaining space on the drive.
- **Logical** = Within the "extended partition", the space within it is "divided" into amounts that the operating system can interact with. Each of these sections operate as if they are a physically separate drive. If there is already a primary partition of "C:\" and possibly an optical drive (Such as a DVD drive), the other sections can be assigned their own drive letter.
- **System versus Boot Partitions** = When a computer only has one operating system on it and the entire volume is utilized both the system and boot partitions may exist in the same location. When there are multiple operating systems at least one will contain a system partition which controls the remaining volumes. The following are some elements which make the different partition unique:
  - o **System Partition** = This section holds files such as the Boot Configuration Data (BCD) required for Windows to turn on. It will not be indicated by letter and is normally not accessed by a user in any way unless modifications of multiple operating systems is desired.
  - o **Boot Partition** = This is where all the Windows installation files are installed such as the root directory, drivers, etc.

MBR Versus UEFI:

The major limitation of MBR partitions is in the size. The largest partition or drive which can be supported by MBR partitions is up to about 2 Terabytes. The graphic below is a good example of partitioning using MBR:

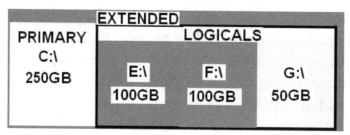

500GB DRIVE

When using systems with drives larger than 2 Terabytes, GPT partitions are required (Globally-Unique-Identifier Partition Table). It is possible to create and modify partitions during a windows installation or even after the operating system has been installed. There are many software utilities which can be purchased on the windows utility "Disk Management" can be used as pictured below:

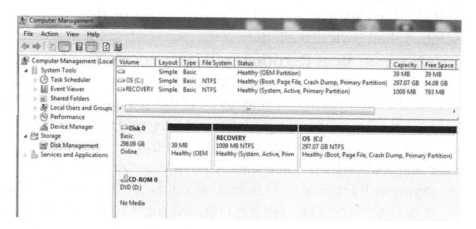

Files and Systems used to Initialize Windows Boot-up:

In this text we will not go into detail about operating systems prior to Windows 7 but there is value in mentioning various files and utilities which allows the Windows operating systems to function. The information is essential because there have been various evolutions and modifications in Microsoft-based operating systems which are often mentioned in certification examinations, texts and other legacy documentation. Also, there is great potential in encountering older operating systems where knowledge of specific files may be helpful. The knowledge might be of particularly advantage when working with operating systems ranging from Windows NT through XP and even implementations of Windows Server 2003.

- **NTLDR (New Technology Loader)** = A collection of files which initialized operating systems on legacy computers allowing Windows to load. In addition, it would allow different versions of Windows and other operating systems such as Linux and DOS to exist on a single computer. For NTLDR to properly operate there also had to be the existence of other files on the volume or drive such as "bootmgr", "winload.exe", "bootsect.dos", "ntdetect.com" and "ntoskrnl.exe". After NTLDR initialized the appropriate files "Boot.ini" would activate. If there was only one operating system detected on the computer it initialize. If there were multiple operating systems the "boot loader menu" would display them as well as which one would automatically load if no selection was made after particular amount of time. In addition, specific information about the operating systems would be displayed related to the name, volume location and default operating system on the computer. Subsequent installations of additional operating system would create another entry in the "Boot.ini". If multiple operating systems are installed subsequent entries and statements are inserted with the most recent operating system being set as a default after the timeout has elapsed. The following sections below are examples of what might appear in a boot menu:
  - [boot loader]
  - timeout=45
  - default=multi(0)disk(0)rdisk(0)partition(1)\WINDOWS
  - [operating systems]
  - multi(0)disk(0)rdisk(0)partition(1)\WINDOWS="Microsoft Windows XP Professional" /fastdetect
  - multi(0)disk(0)rdisk(0)partition(2)\WINNT="Microsoft Windows 2003 Professional" /fastdetect

It is possible to manipulate the entries and options displayed in the boot menu by using the "Control Panel" or the "Boot.cfg" utility. Some of the options that can be manipulated include the following:
  - Descriptive name of the operating system.

- Order the operating systems appear in the menu.
- Default timeout value before a specific operating system engages.

- **Windows Boot Manager** = Windows Boot Manager (Bootmgr) allows a Windows computer system to possess many different operating systems securely without interfering with one another. The boot manager interface not only allows the use of operating systems such as Windows 7 through Windows 10 but it also supports server operating systems such as Server 2008 – 2016 and as well as Linux. Previously operating systems such as Windows NT, 98 and XP utilized "NTLDR" and "Boot.ini" to load up operating systems. The newer implementation of Windows Boot Manager is a combination of three files entitled "Bootmgr.exe" "Winload.exe" and "Winresume.exe". The storage system for these files is known as the "Boot Configuration Data (BCD)" and is edited or controlled thru the use of a utility known as "BCDEdit.exe".

- **Modifying Windows Boot Options:**
  - Using "MSConfig" or "BCDEdit" it is possible to customize the way a windows computer turns on as well as which operating system loads if the computer has multiple operating systems on it. Both utilities require administrative privileges of the user. Within BCDEdit, it is possible to display a number of examples and suggestions for the use of the utility by typing "bcdedit /?" at a command prompt such as in the following example:

```
Administrator: Command Prompt

Microsoft Windows [Version 10.0.17134.885]
(c) 2018 Microsoft Corporation. All rights reserved.

C:\WINDOWS\system32>bcdedit /?

BCDEDIT - Boot Configuration Data Store Editor

The Bcdedit.exe command-line tool modifies the boot configuration data store.
The boot configuration data store contains boot configuration parameters and
controls how the operating system is booted. These parameters were previously
in the Boot.ini file (in BIOS-based operating systems) or in the nonvolatile
RAM entries (in Extensible Firmware Interface-based operating systems). You can
use Bcdedit.exe to add, delete, edit, and append entries in the boot
configuration data store.

For detailed command and option information, type bcdedit.exe /? <command>. For
example, to display detailed information about the /createstore command, type:

    bcdedit.exe /? /createstore

For an alphabetical list of topics in this help file, run "bcdedit /? TOPICS".

Commands that operate on a store
================================
/store          Used to specify a BCD store other than the current system default.
/createstore    Creates a new and empty boot configuration data store.
/export         Exports the contents of the system store to a file. This file
                can be used later to restore the state of the system store.
```

Within the same command line you can also execute "BCDEdit" without modifiers to display the operating systems on the computer as well as which will load first.

```
C:\WINDOWS\system32>bcdedit

Windows Boot Manager
--------------------
identifier              {bootmgr}
device                  partition=\Device\HarddiskVolume1
description             Windows Boot Manager
locale                  en-US
inherit                 {globalsettings}
default                 {current}
resumeobject            {eff60af7-7bcb-11e8-90e9-e589e1a9ab5d}
displayorder            {current}
toolsdisplayorder       {memdiag}
timeout                 30


Windows Boot Loader
-------------------
identifier              {current}
device                  partition=C:
path                    \WINDOWS\system32\winload.exe
description             Windows 10
locale                  en-US
inherit                 {bootloadersettings}
recoverysequence        {78972139-eac8-11e8-951f-c2df49baa9ad}
displaymessageoverride  Recovery
recoveryenabled         Yes
allowedinmemorysettings 0x15000075
osdevice                partition=C:
systemroot              \WINDOWS
resumeobject            {9e1a9af7-7bcb-11e8-90e9-f49ba1a9bd3c}
nx                      OptIn
bootmenupolicy          Standard
```

Chapter 5
Printer Concepts

Printer Concepts:

One of the most customary devices to accompany a computer system is a printer. There are many types of printers such as "Ink Jet", "Laser", "Plotter" and many more. The focus of this text is not repair and maintenance of printing devices but instead the general focus is on a few methods to connect a computer to a printer. When talking about printers they are often placed in specific categories. There is no overall best printer and each category has its strengths as well as disadvantages. When purchasing a printer it is necessary to consider how many pages will be printed each day, environment which the printer exists, number of users of the printer as well as how much money is available to purchase printer supplies. The following are some of the categories of printers and their associated characteristics:

The following are some terms relative to adding a printer to a computer:

- **Printer Driver** = This term represents the software required to allow an operating system to communicate, manage and control a printer. Some printers have drivers already installed in the Windows operating system so there is no need to add any software. This is primarily the case when using a "USB" connected printer. Other printers which have a number of advanced options may require the use of installation media included with the printer packaging (Often a DVD or must be downloaded from the manufacturers website).

- **Shared Printer** = After a printer is installed, it is possible to allow many devices to access the printer. When a printer is shared, other devices can "Browse" (This means to "Search around a network") to locate any shared printers. More capable computer technicians can use a "UNC" method and access the printer from another computer.

- **Local Printer** = This term indicates that the printer is literally directly connected to the computer which is using the device. This direct connection can be parallel or USB. This is the primary method of printer installation on most personal windows computer.

- **Network Printer** = This indicates that there is a type of network in which the printer is "free standing" without a direct connection to any specific computer. The printer has a method of advertising its presences and allowing devices to connect, install drivers from the printer and utilize it to submit documents for printing. The connections for network printers vary from Wireless, Bluetooth,

Infrared and wired IP address. In large corporate environments, there may actually be a Windows Server which is in charge of dozens of printers. In this way, specific users can be given access or denied access to specific printers. It is also possible to change the order of printing documents, clear documents that are not being printed or just deleting un-wanted print jobs.

- **Dot Matrix Printers** = A dot matrix printer is one of the oldest types related to computers. It is most strongly associated with a "typewriter" because it uses a dry ink ribbon and metal pinheads which press the ribbon into a piece of paper producing an image on the document. This is also one of the only printers which still allows the use of carbon paper often used to produce immediate copies of documents which have signatures or credit card numbers on them. A dot matrix printer traditionally is one of the types that produce the most noise and also has a large number of moving parts including a "tractor feed" mechanism and a flywheel with "teeth" for guide holes in customized paper for use with this type of printer.

- **Inkjet Printer (Or "Bubble-Jet")** = This type of printer uses ink cartridges each having its own "spray nozzle" (Very tiny "cans of spray paint"). Cartridge can be individual or in some printer models there may be four or six cartridges combined into a single unit. When the print job occurs the cartridges move in unison across the piece of paper and each nozzle shoots a very small amount of ink at particular times creating an image as they move. These type of printers are normally the least expensive but have high costs related to print cartridges which often dry-out or individually run out of ink interfering with the other cartridges ability to produce colors produced by mixing the colors.

- **Thermal Printers** = A thermal printer requires paper which is specially treated with chemicals resulting in it being reactive to heat which allows images to be produced wherever a heated print head strikes the paper.

- **Laser Printers** = Probably the most common type of printer used in office environments. Laser printers have high production capacity and can be connected directly to a computer or a network jack which allows hundreds of users access to the same printer. They can be a small as a shoebox or is large as an office desk depending on the manufacturer and options available on the unit. Some of the parts on most laser printers include the photo drum, the toner cartridge, the charging corona and print rollers. Depending on the manufacture of the printer there may be more or less parts but the parts mentioned are the most universal.

Laser Printing Process:

Many computer technician examinations (Particularly CompTIA's "A+" examination) make mention of the steps a laser printer performs in order to put images on a document. The following are some of the terms used in the laser printing process:

1. **Processing** = Data from the sending computer is transferred into RAM on the printer for transmission to the photosensitive drum.
2. **Charging** = The imaging drum receives an electric charge (Between 400 and 600 Volts) moving the toner away from the drum.
3. **Exposing** = A laser draws an image on the drum which deactivates the electrical charge in those specific areas.
4. **Developing** = Ink toner is attracted to the areas on the drum which had been struck by the laser light.
5. **Transferring** = A transfer corona causes the toner ink to be pulled onto the paper above the areas which had the electrical charge changed by the laser.
6. **Fusing** = A heated roller melts the toner ink permanently into an image on the paper.
7. **Cleaning** = The electrical charge is reversed on the drum allowing the toner to fall away and a laser removes all imaging information from the drum.

Chapter 6
What is an "Application", "Program" or "Software"?

What is Software?

Software consists of instruction set created by programmers using many types of languages traditionally called "Computer Code". Software has many different functions and runs on various types of devices ranging from a DVD player to more recognized computer devices. Software can be divided into many different categories such as Operating System Software which operates the computer, Application Software which allows a user to create documents, spreadsheet, send e-mail, view web pages and many other daily technology-related activities and Firmware which allows an operating system to communicate with specific devices such as speakers and printers. The following paragraphs are discussions and illustrations of types of software.

What is Firmware?

Firmware is a software designed to communicate with a specific hardware device such as a hard drive, printer, speaker, DVD drives, scanners, etc. This software is not normally manipulated or changed by the everyday user because it normally serves to interact between an operating system and a device. Firmware is normally stored on ROM and can be altered by a firmware update.

What is Shareware?

Shareware are programs that are offered at no charge by the owner. The free software usually has some type of limitation either with all of the available functions or a specific number of days that the software will operate after which it will lock up and no longer accept user input. The reason the creator offers the software in this manner is the hope that a user finds the program very helpful or the user simply enjoys using the software. Either after the time limit has expired or the user desires a fully-functioning version of the program, the user can make some type of payment to the creator which allows the user full program access.

What are Drivers?

A device driver is a limited group of files or a small program which allows an operating system to communicate with a hardware device such as printers, scanners and optical drives. Drivers are often confused with Firmware but the primary difference is that Firmware exists on ROM while drivers exist in operating systems. Drivers allow hardware to utilize files within operating systems which remove the necessity of each hardware manufacturer to create all the code required to communicate with different operating systems. Without drivers, the computer would not be able to send and receive data correctly to hardware devices, such as a printer.

What are File Types (Extensions)?

There are thousands of different types of files which may appear on a computer system. Some files are run by operating systems, other file types are activated by users and some file types simply indicate the program which was used to create them. Most file types are differentiated by their extension. An extension also can inform an operating system what program to use in order to access a particular file. This is what occurs when you "Double-Click" on a Microsoft Word document, and the computer turns on Microsoft Word. The process of an operating system activating a program which can interact with or view a file type is called "Association". Some well-known extensions are as follows:

- **PDF** = Adobe Reader (Allows display of text files)
- **Xlsx (Xls)** = Microsoft Excel (Spreadsheet Application)
- **Docx (doc)** = Microsoft Word (Word Processor Application)
- **Txt** = Notepad (Extremely limited application for text documents)
- **Jpg** = Joint Picture Experts Group (High-Detail Photo)
- **Gif** = Graphics Interchange Format (Small Size Photo)
- **WAV** = Waveform Audio File Format (Windows Music/Sound file)
- **WMV** = Windows Media Video (Movie file)
- **MPEG** = Moving Picture Experts Group (Movie file)

Utilizing "Batch Files":

In computer technology, there are a number of methods performing tasks and actions. Methods of turning on programs vary between different applications and tasks. The most commonly used method of activating programs presently is using "icons" or "buttons" on the start menu or desktop area. What is not well known is that each button executes dozens of actions on the CLI of the operating system. It is possible to combine hundreds of commands and have them all performed by using a click on an icon which is associated with a file launched by a single word input in the operating systems CLI. The process of using a single file to perform multiple tasks is often called "Scripting". "Scripting" comes in a large variety of formats ranging from "Visual Basic (VB)" and "Java Script". In the area of computer technology and computer repair, the script type called "Batch Files" are often used.

Batch files can be used to allow a computer or application to perform a number of commands after a user has activated a single file. The file extension for a batch file is "<filename>.BAT". The file might be activated by using an icon or using a command thru the CLI. When using the CLI, there is a requirement to making the command usable from various areas. The following are options for running a batch file from the CLI (Note: These options are mentioned for reference but not utilized in this text):

Execute the command from the same directory in which the batch file exists. Create or modify a file called the "Autoexec.bat" to load the directory path of the batch file into memory upon computer startup. If there was a batch file called inside of a number of sub-directories entitled "getpay.bat" it would be possible to place the following statements within the autoexec.bat in order to utilize the command from any CLI location:

- **Path=C:\myscripts\mybatches("Getpay.bat" is located inside of this directory.)**

The following is a task which could be performed by the batch file. The file has the purpose of connecting to a computer and activating a file called "Payroll.xls":

- **C:** (Make the CLI concentrate on the "C:\>")
- **CD** (Makes the CLI concentrate on the Root of the directory.)
- **Net Use X:** \\Server01\Staff (Connects the present operating system to a directory entitled "Staff" within a computer called "Server01").
- **X:** (Make the CLI concentrate on the "X:\>")
- **CD staff** (Makes the CLI concentrate on the directory "staff".)
- **Payroll.xls** (Opens the file which now displays on the computer which activated the batch file).

What is a "Software Utility"?

Utilities are used for various maintenance, status check and repair tasks. A utility is normally smaller in size than traditional applications and have a purpose which is normally related to a single function of an operating system, hardware component or different application. Example of a utility might be some of the following:

- **Antivirus** = Protects computer against programs which might cause damage or steal data.
- **System Restore** = Allows computer's condition to be protected in case operating system becomes inoperative.
- **Document Backup** = Additional copies of important documents in case originals are lost or damaged.
- **Hard Drive Repair** = Re-arranges information on sections of hard drive for improved performance, dependability and faster data access.
- **Magnifier** = Enhances and increases the size of icons, windows and fonts on screen for easier viewing for vision impaired users.
- **Text-To-Speech** = Computers literally reads text on screen and outputs the words audibly via speakers.
- **Desktop Gadgets** = Customized icons which display various areas of interests (i.e., Computer Statistics, Local Weather, Traffic Reports, Twitter Feeds, etc.).
- **Screen Saver** = Causes screen to display various images when computer is not in use such as Photo Albums, Poems, Museum Artwork, etc.

What is an "Application" versus a "Program"?

These two terms often cause confusion. Depending on your level of expertise or actual job, there is only a small difference between the two. A debate about the two terms is really a waste of time but if you need a really "weak" definition of either, the following elements can be applied. A program would be code or a language such as C++, Java, Alice, Visual Basic, etc. These are tools used to create software. An application is software designed to perform functions, tasks, or processes which will produce some type of object, data or process result. The data or process result could be graphics (Pictures), text, music, video and many other elements in computer technology. Applications are controlled by a user's direct interaction with a computer and have no responsibility of running the actual computer. Presently, there are hundreds of applications available for computers which give people the ability to create and manipulate an almost limitless list of products. Applications are utilized in multiple areas of education, business, art, music, publishing, architecture, the list goes on forever. The following are some examples of well-known applications:

- **Microsoft Word** = Word Processor application allows the creation of typed documents.
- **Halo** = Action "first-person vantage point" video game simulating soldiers in the future
- **PeachTree** = Spreadsheet application used in accounting, databases and graph creation.
- **Google Chrome** = Allows viewing of websites, videos, and limited control of network devices.
- **Adobe Photoshop** = Used to alter, enhance and create pictures and other photography related materials.
- **Call of Duty** = Action "first-person vantage point" video game simulating soldiers in past wars, present contemporary conflicts and future wars.
- **Outlook** = Performs E-mail, scheduling, contact list (Phonebook) and calendar functions.

Many times, multiple programs are sold in "collections" called "Suites". This is a method manufactures use to increase the possibility of users selecting more than one of their products in the future. For example, if a person works in the banking field, they may need both spreadsheet and word processing applications. In this scenario, the user may select to purchase Microsoft Word and Peachtree. It is possible however to purchase the "Microsoft Office Suite" instead which includes Microsoft Word for word processing and a spreadsheet application called "Excel". In this way, the user can save money by only purchasing what looks like a single program. The advantage to Microsoft is that if the user starts using Excel, it is highly probable that the user will continue to use future versions of Excel as well as encourage their co-workers to use the program.

How does a person get Access to Software?

In the field of server technology is important to practice using various types of software. Normally, there are many options available for companies such as Microsoft, Oracle and even Apple. When a person training is a student, the options are extremely large. Essentially, many companies will provide software to students for free or at an extremely reduced price. I know of students who were able to acquire fully-functioning versions of almost all of the Microsoft Office Suite as well as many of the server and workstation related operating systems at no cost to them. The first thing someone might think is that the software is "Pirated" (Essentially stolen without paying for it). Please relax. This is not case with the software I mention. The software is fully legal and obtained from the original vendor such as Microsoft. How are the students able to acquire the software, you ask? Really simple, Microsoft wants you to sell it for them!

Essentially, Microsoft will provide specific applications and operating systems to a student enrolled in any college or training institution. The primary requirement is to register with an e-mail account which reflects an approved existing educational facility. Microsoft is allowing students to acquire applications and operating systems at no charge in order to increase their potential for future sales. The philosophy is that if students learn how to use Microsoft based applications and operating systems, in the future that student might gain a job in which they can make recommendation of what software to purchase for the company of which they are employed. Most people purchase software that they are experienced with using. In the event that you have been using Microsoft Office products for three or four years, there is a great potential that you will recommend the purchase of the same software in the future. In this process, Microsoft may have given a student a software package which costs $300.00. If that same student who has now graduated, purchases the software for 10 people in a company. Microsoft will now earn $3,000.00. This has been a marketing strategy Microsoft has used for over 10 years and it is one of primary reasons Microsoft Word is used by so many companies.

There are a number of websites which offer access to applications, and operating systems. Some are what are called "Third-Party Vendors" (Not the original company which created or owns the software as opposed to companies such as Microsoft and Apple). The following are some of the websites which provide access to software at different prices and sometimes free as of the publication date of this textbook:

- **Microsoft Azure = Database and Server Software:**
    - https://azure.microsoft.com/en-us/services/virtual-machines/
    - https://azure.microsoft.com/en-us/free/services/virtual-machines/
- **Microsoft Evaluation Center = Various Server ISO's and VM's:**
    - https://www.microsoft.com/en-us/evalcenter/evaluate-windows-server-2016
- **Adobe Downloads** = http://www.adobe.com/downloads.html
- **Apple Downloads** = https://support.apple.com/downloads

Define "Software/Hardware Requirements".

When installing software on computers, it is very important to know the capabilities of that computer. Questions concerning how much RAM the computer can use, what type of video card is installed and other issues such as hard drive space, operating system, etc. Installing an incompatible operating system on a computer is normally a fatal operation which can result in the loss of important data or the entire functioning ability of the computer. In order to compensate for this, all software comes with two lists which outlines what a computer will need to run the software. The list comes in two forms:

- **Minimum Specifications** = These standards will allow the installation of the software with some limitations or restrictions. The limitations and restrictions could be the speed in which the software will operate or specific tasks which may be unavailable. If it is "video editing" program which allows new sounds to be recorded, it would require a microphone of some type. If the computer has no microphone, the other functions of the software will still operate, but no live recording will take place. In addition to not being able to perform specific operations, other functions and processes could take minutes (Or literally "hours") to complete due to limited RAM or CPU capabilities. Adhering to the "Minimum Specifications" often results in poor performance and dissatisfaction in the software (Or the computer).
- **Recommended Specifications** = These are the standards which were used to test the software in various stages of its development.

In addition, when using the recommended specifications, results, times, and expectations have been confirmed. Exceeding the recommended specifications often have the benefit of greater enhancement of the software. When working on businesses and corporate servers, it is always best practice to exceed the recommended specifications.

Chapter 7
What is an Operating System?

Well-Known Operating Systems:

This is the software which allows control and modification of hardware on computerized devices. To use the human body as a comparison, the operating system is like the "spirit" which guides activities or the "unconscious" functions such as breathing, eye blinking or heartbeat. Operating systems are always working anytime a computer is turned on, regardless if a person is interacting with the unit. Although there are many operating systems in existence today, some of the most well-known are Unix, Microsoft Windows, the Mac OS and Linux. The operating system performs functions such as moving data between parts inside the computer such as the hard drive, RAM and or the internet connection. Every activity which can be performed is executed by the operating system. Every time a key is pressed, the operating system performs actions. All programs (Also called "Applications") are also maintained and controlled by the operating system allowing each of them to share data streams and storage space. All data stored on a computer is arranged by the operating system as well as communicating with parts outside of the computer such as speakers, monitor and printer. The operating system also provides a method for a user to interact with the computer called a "User Interface (Also called "UI")". The User Interface on most computer have various names such as GUI (Graphical User Interface), WebUI (Web User Interface) and CLI (Command Line Interface). The discussions within this text will include aspects of all three methods. Some well-known operating systems would include the following:

- **Microsoft Windows** = Residing on what has been estimated at over 80% of the computers in the world, "Windows" is a collection of operating systems for desktops, laptops, servers and even cellphones. Versions of Windows begin being utilized near about 1985 and utilize a graphical user interface with access to command line functions. Although there are many different versions of the Windows operating system, the primary division appear as either a "client/workstation" or "server" implementations. "Client" operating systems are designed for everyday personal use or in office environments. Examples of client versions of operating systems would be "Windows XP", "Windows 7 thru 10". Client operating systems are designed to utilize applications such as "Microsoft Word" and play computer games. "Server" platforms are optimized for multi-user access and data-conversion speeds such as streaming video like "Netflix" or photo exchange such as "Facebook".

- **Unix** = Unix is a proprietary operating system commonly used on internet servers, workstations and PCs by Solaris, Intel, HP etc. Unix is a family of multitasking, multiuser computer operating systems that derive from the original AT&T Unix, developed between 1967 and the early 1970's at the Bell Labs research center by Ken Thompson, Dennis Ritchie, and others. Unix is presently a world-wide known operating system often used on large single location computers often known as "mainframes" and "Super Computers". Unix operating systems require a strong knowledge of command line operations and directory structure. Although there are GUI distributions, the primary control source is via the CLI. The Unix OS is often a very expensive operating system and many distributions require very specific computer components for it to function. Due to these requirements of the operating system, it is primarily used by organizations such as international banks, department of defense, banks and airlines for their network communications and infrastructure.

- **Linux** = A programmer named "Linus Torvalds" primarily create the essential core files (Often called the "Linux kernel") based on another operating system called "Unix". Torvalds had the belief that technology and operating systems should be free for anyone who is interested so did not patent the files and offered them as "open-source" which means the files can be distributed at no cost and modified by anyone around the world. Due to the operating system being "open-source", there are hundreds of different versions with multiple commands and associated graphical user interfaces. Due to the low cost (Or "No cost") of this operating system, it is used in a multitude of environments to reduce the cost of creating servers. In addition, the default command structures and directories are configured very similarly to the Unix operating system which allows a user to practice Unix functions on a more affordable operating system.

- **Mac OS** = The Mac OS is the source program created by Apple to control what was once called "Macintosh" computers. Originally, Apple computers hosted an operating system totally created by apple, but now the company has moved to an implementation of "Unix" which they now market as "The Mac OS". The company

Apple has evolved and is now the world's greatest produce of cellphones related to the "IPhone" line of smartphones. Similar to Windows operating systems there are multiple versions of the Mac OS, often based upon the year of release. Some versions would be Lion, Yosemite, Kodiak, Puma, Panther and Leopard. In addition, the Mac OS also allows a graphical user interface to control windows and icons to manipulate programs and features of the computer.

Mobile Device Operating Systems (Smart Phones and Tablets):

Although not computers, Smart phones (Which are different from the term "Cellphones" which are simply devices with limited capabilities such as only making phone calls, text messages and perhaps camera features), tablets and Netbooks also have operating systems. Mobile devices do not have any of the traditional operating systems listed previously in this book but they have reduced versions or proprietary (Meaning specialized and owned by the manufacturer) operating systems. Operating systems on smartphones are not created for manipulation by users. The priority for smartphone operating systems is to allow the user to interact with the Internet, E-mail, global positioning systems (GPS) and telephone exchange service for the country to which the smartphone exists. There are many other applications available for smartphones but not on the same level as desktop or laptop computers. Traditional computers are classified as a "Utility (A device used to produce, create and manipulate data)". Mobile devices such as smartphones are usually limited to accessing or exchanging data. Some names for the operating systems on mobile devices would include the Apple IOS for IPhones or Android operating system on many smartphones created by Samsung.

Windows Graphical User Interface (GUI):

In the early 1980's it was required for computer operators to always have an understanding of the storage method used by a computer. Today, most users of Windows computers have no idea that there is a thing called an "operating system" which is arranged like a file cabinet with many "drawers" holding "directories" which also hold "sub-directories" which end with a collection of "files". This method of organizing data and programs on computers is called a "Directory Structure".

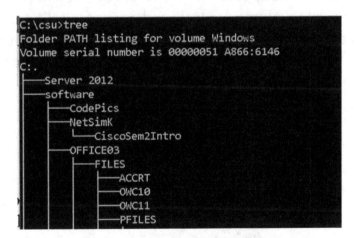

Oftentimes, the training for operating computers became an issue so computer programmers began to investigate methods to make interacting with a computer less complicated. After years of experiments, operating systems began to come with the ability to perform CLI commands without ever knowing any of them. This revolutionary method of communicating and controlling with computers became known as using a Graphical User Interface (Often abbreviated in writing as "GUI" and verbally by using the word "Goo-eee").

In many cases, computer users no longer had to even use the keyboard. Depending on the computer being used, most of the daily required functions could now be performed by simply using a mouse and "clicking" on a picture on the display. These "pictures" are now referred to as "Icons" or "Buttons". As mentioned earlier, the total collection of items which can be utilized makeup a "Graphical User Interface (Known as a "GUI" and usually pronounced as "Goo-ey")". The GUI was created to remove the need to know CLI commands to activate and operate computer systems. Using a GUI allows symbols called "icons" on a computer screen to be activated via clicking a mouse or keyboard button. These icons are directly associated with commands which are run in the background by the operating system. In addition, many commonly used functions can be displayed on a "menu" screen via clicking additional buttons on a mouse. In the world of Windows Computing, the following are items used by many computer operators:

- **Desktop** = This is the primary area to access programs when a windows computer boots. It includes many icons which activate programs as well as sections which display active programs, present time and date, volume controls and many other features convenient for users. The desktop can also be "personalized" for a user to display favorite photos, websites, weather displays, calendars, and many other items.

- **Start Menu/Button** = This is the core area to locate and activate programs on a computer. Recently used applications, newly installed programs and a feature which allows a user to search for files exist in this area. With the advent of Windows 8 and 10, the "button" aspect of this area has many different styles which can be activated. This "Shell" in the illustration is only one of the many.

  In addition, there are also technical-related icons such as the command line interface, Windows Help and Support and System tools.

- **Search Programs and Files (Also called the "Run" Option)** = Originally, this area allowed a technician to utilize CLI functions, one of those being searching the operating system for files lost by a user. As time progressed, Microsoft noticed non-technical users often performed the function of searching for files so they enhanced the area to allow faster and more efficient searches for files based on name, date of creation, size of file, type of file and many other attributes. The original technical functions are still enabled in this area however, so programs can be launched or network resources can be typed in various formats such as using a "UNC".

- **Recycle Bin** = This area is the default place which stores files if they have been deleted from other areas of the computer. Think of it as a "safety feature" in case you accidently delete a file and later decide you needed. If a file is deleted, it literally stays in this area until about 85% of the actual space on a computer's hard drive (Area which stores files long-term) is used, then data in the Recycle Bin will begin to erase files, starting with the older files first.

- **Task Bar** = This is the bar which appears at the bottom of most Windows desktops. It displays shortcuts for often used programs, programs active on the computer, network connections, volume controls, calendars, and many other items. Although traditionally at the bottom, the Taskbar can be moved around to any edge of the display and also resized or hidden from view. The Taskbar can also be "personalized" with icons, widgets and gadgets.

- **Windows Explorer (Displays Directories or "Folders")** = This interface allows a GUI display of the directory (Often called "Folders" in GUI terms) within a computer system. The interface has many display options such as mini-pictures of photos called "Thumbnails", "Date of Creation", "Large Icon", "File Preview" windows, and many more. The Explorer window can also be re-positioned, and resized for better view of items contained within the present window.

- **Title Bar** = This area identifies the application presently active as well as the name of the directory being viewed. The Title bar is found both in the windows operating system as well as many programs. It is also possible to use the Title Bar to reposition the entire window of a program or directory in a different location on the desktop in the event the view of another window is obscured.
- **Sizing Buttons** = These icons appear on the far right of a title bar. They are control features which allow you to quickly alter the

characteristics of a displayed window. The following are the functions of each button:

- o **Minimize** = Will shrink an entire window and only display its presence on the Task Bar. To return the window to its previous size and location, the icon representing the minimized window need only be "double-clicked".
- o **Restore (Full or Down)** = Depending on the previous stage of an explorer window, this button provides two functions. Either it will make the window encompass the entire area available for display on a monitor, or; the button will return window taking up the entire display to the previous size and location on the desktop.
- **Exit/Close** = Depending on the window in which the buttons are located, this icon will either remove one active document from a number of documents running in an application from view, or totally turn off a running program.
- **File Menu** = These icons appear as "words" beneath the Title bar and above the detail area of most explorer windows. Each icon gives access to command menu's relevant to whichever explorer window to which it is associated. In the window displayed, you see the options "File", "Computer" and "View". The File menu options will change depending on the window or the application. When using the present version of Microsoft Word, the File Menu reads "File", "Insert", "Page Layout" and a few more items particular to that application.

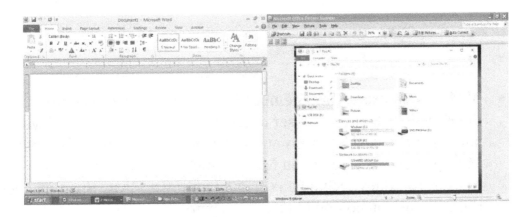

- **Control Panel** = This area allows access to devices, programs, customizations and system settings for the operating system. It is possible from here to configure network settings, power settings and many more features. Another aspect is to use this area to establish security, anti-virus and system update settings.

- **Computer Management** = This is a well-known interface created by Microsoft to allow a technician quick access to a number of operating system controls. There are hundreds of controllable aspects of a Windows computer. Computer Management allows you to both view and customize different elements of a computer's environment.

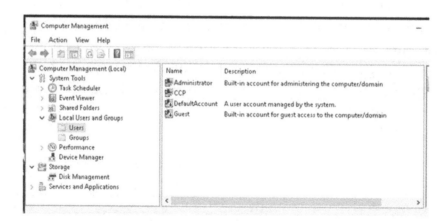

- **MMC (Microsoft Management Console)** = This is a control interface which allows a user to create a "Control Interface" with particular selected Snap-ins and Extensions. Actually, "Computer Management" is actually an MMC which was customized by Microsoft. Many technicians create their own MMC Snap-ins they routinely use on computers during repairs.

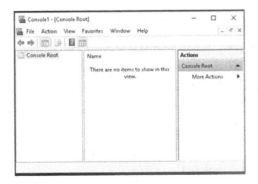

- **MMC Snap-In** = This is a term used to describe the control interfaces which appear in an MMC such as Computer Management. The items such as "Local Users and Groups", "Services" and "Shares" are just a few of the many. Various Snap-ins can be loaded into most MMC's.
- **MMC Extension** = In relation to an MMC, an extension is the end of a Snap-in. It is the place of the interface in which there are no additional sub-features. An example of a Snap-in would be "Services". Many different Snap-ins have a multitude of Extensions.

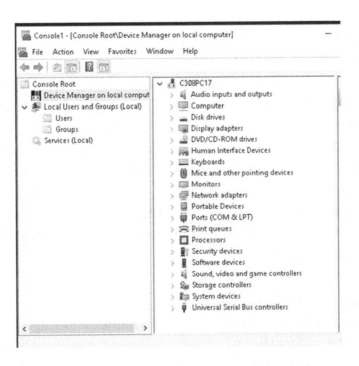

- **Local Users and Groups** = This is a common feature within Computer Management. This allows the creation of different users on a single computer. This gives the benefit of allowing each user to have their own "design" to the Desktop area as well as creating different sections for users to store their documents, pictures and other files. Within "Local Users and Groups" some users (Such as "Parents") will be "in charge" of the computers and can make any changes possible. Other users (Such as "Children") should be prohibited from making changes. In order to accomplish this, there are "Groups" setup on most operating systems. Group names and abilities include the following:

- **Administrator** = Total control of the computer system.
- **User** = Only offers ability to use programs but not make any system-wide changes.
- **Power User** = Allows minor changes to computer which will not affect the overall function of the operating system.

What is a Web User Interface (WebUI)?

This interface allows a user to access a computer or network device by using an application called a "Browser" which is normally used to view web pages on the internet. Examples of browsers are "Internet Explorer", "Google Chrome" and "Firefox". It is somewhat of a "blend" between a "GUI" and a "Browser Application". The computer or device must have an operating IP address and software which will convert icon clicks into commands performed on the device. Many high-level network devices called "Switches" and "Routers" have the capability to be controlled via a WebUI. This method is mentioned due to it being a standard but will not be illustrated in this text.

The Command Line Interface (CLI):

This is an interface which requires an in-depth understanding of the structure of operating systems. In order to activate elements and functions in the operating system, a user is required to type out the exact word which initiates a function. Spelling must be perfect in order to manipulate a CLI operating system. Many present day operating systems offer access to the CLI. On Windows-based operating systems the CLI is often confused with an operating system which is no longer used called "DOS (Short for "Disk Operating System")". Below is an example of using a CLI to ascertain the network settings being used by a computer.

One of the most misunderstood options available on operating is entitled the **"Command Line Interface"** normally abbreviated as "CLI". Many persons who have some knowledge of computers will refer to this access method as "DOS". The "look" of "DOS" and the "CLI" are very similar. Below is a DOS screen. Notice the top does not have a title bar.

Notice that when using the Windows CLI, there is a Title Bar at the top:

"DOS (Disk Operating System)" is an extremely outdated operating system used by Microsoft between 1980 and 1998. Essentially, the operating system DOS used "command-words" to perform functions. If a user did not understand the correct format for the "words" they would be unable to utilize a computer. About 1993, one of the first GUI's (Graphical User Interface) entitled "Windows for Workgroups", was produced. This GUI was installed on top of DOS which allowed functions to be performed using pictures referred to as "icons" and "buttons". The buttons interacted with DOS as a control feature. DOS was replaced by Windows 98 but the ability to use command line was retained using the command "command" and/or "cmd" in the "Search" field of a "Start Menu". Most technicians referred to the "search" field as the "Run" option.

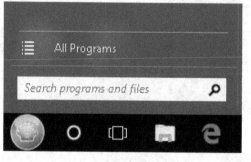

In the field of computer/server technology, there are many CLI functions used. One of the reasons which supports CLI functions is that the command words do not often change. The "buttons" and "icons" normally change between operating systems or even between different versions of the same operating systems. The command "ping" for example is the same on Linux, Unix, Windows and even the Cisco Router and Switch operating systems. All are run from a CLI. The following are some of the more well-known CLI commands performed on Windows:

- **Dir** = Displays the contents of the directory presently being viewed.
- **Cls** = Removes previous command results from the CLI.
- **Cd** = Redirects the focus of the command prompt (i.e., "C:\Windows\System32>") to a directory within the present directory.
- **cd** = Redirects the focus of the command prompt (i.e., "C:\Windows\System32>") to the root (Top) of the drive being viewed.

- **cd ..** = Redirects the focus of the command prompt (i.e., "C:\Windows\System32>") back one level to the previous or containing directory.
- **Mkdir <name>** = Creates a directory that is named in the command.
- **Rmdir <name>** = Eliminates a directory that is named in the command.
- **Notepad** = This command will turn on the program "Notepad".
- **Calc** = This command will activate the Microsoft Calculator (If it is installed).
- **MSPaint** = This command will activate Microsoft Paint (If installed).
- **Tree** = This command will display the relationship between directories and subdirectories in a linked-line format **(Notice: The results of this command could take a few minutes to complete).**
- **"Tree /p" or "Dir /p"** = Displays a few lines of the results of the command with a pause. Pressing any key on the keyboard will allow the display of files and directories to continue with pauses until the complete results of the command are complete.

The following are some practical applications of some CLI commands. All start with accessing the run option in "Search Programs and Files". Many of the examples listed will be evaluated later in this book. Feel free to experiment with them before the listed exercises, they will not damage your computer. Although, you might want to do them on a computer that is not important because it will reduce the computers security:

- **Running a program like "notepad":**
  - ➢ C: (Make the CLI concentrate on the "C:\>")
  - ➢ CD\ (Makes the CLI concentrated on the Root of the directory.)
  - ➢ Notepad (Starts the Notepad application)
- **Running a program like the Windows "Calculator":**
  - ➢ C: (Make the CLI concentrate on the "C:\>")
  - ➢ CD\ (Makes the CLI concentrated on the Root of the directory.)
  - ➢ Calc (Starts the "Calculator" application).
- **Creating a new directory called "Staff" inside of "C:\>" drive:**
  - ➢ C: (Make the CLI concentrate on the "C:\>")
  - ➢ CD\ (Makes the CLI concentrated on the Root of the directory.)
  - ➢ Mkdir staff

- **Restarting a Computer:**
  - C: (Make the CLI concentrate on the "C:\>")
  - CD\ (Makes the CLI concentrated on the Root of the directory.)
  - Shutdown /r (Turns off the system after all processes normally close)
- **Shutting down a Computer:**
  - C: (Make the CLI concentrate on the "C:\>")
  - CD\ (Makes the CLI concentrated on the Root of the directory.)
  - Shutdown /s (Turns off the system after all processes normally close)

Chapter 8
CyberCriminals and Viruses

"Hackers" versus "Crackers":

There are many conversations in the cyber-security and computer world in reference to the term "Hackers" and also the lesser-known term of "Crackers". Although there is no need to go into intense detail on the similarities and differences in the terms, it is appropriate to give them mention in a book which examines computer technology. Both terms are attempting to define experts in the computer field who have a great understanding of computer language (Often called "computer code") and computer communication software (Often called "protocols"). Utilizing this knowledge, these computer experts can participate in two distinct activities:

- **"Hacker"** = Identify and exploit areas in which a computer or network system can be damaged or compromised. These persons often work for businesses which create options for computer security or antivirus software. Their goal is to assure the continued operation of a business and to safeguard all data maintained and services provided by the business or company. Computer experts in this area are also often called "White Hats".
- **"Cracker"** = Participate in compromising or damaging computers and other network devices. The term originated from the term "Safe Cracker" (Person who would rob vaults in banks, stores and other businesses). Primarily working as "contractors" or "individual/group" entities, they have the goal of participating in malicious activities concerning computer data, services or operation. In contrast with hackers, they are often referred to as "Black Hats". Examples of malicious activities would include the following:
  - o Stopping or destroying computer data using virus or network attacks (Trojans, phishing, DoS, etc.).
  - o Accessing and distributing confidential data (Movies, credit card and personal data, etc.).
  - o Stopping an internet business from being accessed by users (i.e., Netflix, Sony PlayStation, etc.).

Although, there is a distinction made between "Hackers" and "Crackers", their abilities are the same but their motives define their classification. Depending on the situation and affiliations, they could be the "good guys" or the "bad guys" depending on the perspective and the matter at hand. There are many movies which attempt to display the story of the "person who hacks into a computer system and later gains a really good job in the computer field." Although this is a possibility, remember always that accessing computer data without appropriate authorization and approval may be viewed as a crime punishable by termination or prison time. In the event you are involved accessing computer data for yourself or a company, make sure you are represented by a lawyer. Protect yourself at all times.

What is a "Computer Virus" or "Malware"?

A virus is a program which was created to carry out malicious activities on a computer. Literally a programmer used computer code to create a set of instructions which will negatively affect a computer or the user on a computer. The negative effect could be stealing data, stopping the use of a computer or file and even destroying the operating systems or the hardware on a computer. Viruses come in multiple forms but they all have at least two elements in common which are damaging effect and ability to replicate (Duplicate itself in different places).

Similar to a disease that can be spread from person-to-person by contact, a computer virus spreads between computer systems using some type of transmission or common contact area such as a file, storage area (Flashdrive, SD card, Website, etc.) or even an e-mail. All viruses do not immediately attack a computer or user. Often time, many viruses stay inactive on a system until the user performs a specific activity or a "timer" of some type activates the virus. The only way to protect your computer from virus attacks is to think about it like your home and use the same protections:

- **Turn away unknown strangers at your door** = If an e-mail comes to you that you do not recognize, delete it. Do not open it.
- **Keep doors locked when away and turn on security system** = Install Firewall and Antivirus software to stop virus from coming in via websites and documents as well as removing those which made it past the firewalls.
- **Always know your neighbors** = Be aware of the actual identities of people who send or exchange data with your computer. Keep your antivirus system up to date.

There are many antivirus utilities on the market. There is no "best one" but keep in mind, "The more locks you have on your door, the more difficult it will be for the thief". My analogy here is that the more you spend on an antivirus, the greater protection it offers. There is a balance, however. The higher the level of antivirus and firewall you have on your computer, the more resources it will use (Such as the CPU and RAM). If you place an expensive antivirus program on a cheap computer, the computer will operate extremely slowly. Match your antivirus with the abilities on your computer (Commonly referred to as the "Requirements" or "Specifications") to assure that the antivirus you install will not affect your computer worse than actually having a virus. The following are some types and categories of viruses:

- **Spyware** = This term is used to describe software which is installed without a computer owner's permission in order to gather private information and make it available to the owner of the spyware (Often by reporting the data in the form of an e-mail). The information could include, internet activities, visited websites, keystrokes (also called "keylogging"), saved documents and passwords. Similar to Spyware is a variant called "Adware" which will cause a computer browser homepage to change or initiate visiting unknown websites without the users request or display commercials randomly on a computer. The most well-known cause of adware is when a user attempts to download a "free" software not knowing that the condition is the installation of software which will force your browser to use a search engine not selected by you.

- **Trojan** = This virus is created to look innocent. Often it will look like a normal document such as a "docx" or "pdf". It is also often disguised as an e-mail attachment. Traditionally, Trojans do not replicate automatically and require a user to perform some type of activity to activate them. Once activated by a user, a Trojan virus can perform a number of different attacks on a computer system such as recording the keys pressed on a keyboard, deleting files, changing filenames or making files invisible (Or what we call "Hidden").

- **Worm** = Worms travel between computers in order to send copies of data back to the creator of the Worm. Normally this data is credit cards, social security numbers, customer databases, etc. The data is often deposited on a website or contained in a hidden e-mail. Worms often hide their existence and create "backdoors (Method of accessing an operating system or device without the owners' knowledge)" which a malicious program can utilize to continue to compromise data records and systems. An important aspect involving a Worm is that is normally "self-replicating" which means that it copies itself and travels between computers systems without the intervention of a programmer. Once launched on a computer, until erased, a Worm is totally self-sufficient.

- **Macro** = The name for this virus originates from the function available in programs to automatically perform a number of tasks after activating a key combination or clicking on a single icon. When the macro is a virus, however, the tasks could include inserting lines of text in the header or footer of every document printed. A macro virus installs itself into other programs and will replicate itself into any files or documents created with that particular program. Another example would be when an e-mail is sent to a user, commercials or advertisement from the creator of the Macro virus would also be sent to the recipient.

- **Hijackware (Also called "Redirection Malware")** = This type of virus modifies the settings of internet browsers such as Internet Explorer, Google Chrome and Firefox. The results of getting Hijackware are evident when a user's internet search is randomly redirected to Web sites other than those for which were being searched. Often time, the home page of the user or the default search engine is also changed. Unknown bookmarks, pornographic pop-ups and random commercials are often symptoms of Hijackware. There have been a number of versions of Hijackware which totally locks a computer and attempts to force the user to send money to the creator of the virus in order to be given an unlock code. Most often, the unlock code is never sent and the data as well as the money paid is forever lost.

- **Rootkits** = Utilities and software often used for legal purposes such as investigations involving computers and other network devices. They are also used for illegal activities related to accessing and compromising data. Rootkits come in many forms such as the following:
    - Provide a criminal continual access to files within a computer without the owner's knowledge.
    - Allows a criminal to have "Administrator" rights on a computer.
    - Records keystrokes, activities and behaviors performed on a computer to be stored for later access and review.
    - Hides its presence from all users on that particular computer.
    - Allows remote control of the computer (Called "Remote Access").

o Some Rootkit names are as follows:
  - ➤ **Careto** = Used to spy on the activities of computer users.
  - ➤ **Dexter** = Used to steal credit card and other personal information.
  - ➤ **Stuxnet** = Used to manipulate the behavior of circuitry controlling centrifuges used in the processing nuclear materials.
  - ➤ **Mebroot** = Allows a remote control of a computer in order to manipulate files.

Active System Attack Explanations:

In addition to the dangers of viruses, there are persons who use their knowledge of computer code and software to create applications to actively attack and disable computers and entire networks. These individuals can literally access a computer system and attempt to compromise computer settings. A more popular method is to create software which will automatically attack computers without user intervention. The following are some of the types and categories of Active System Attacks:

- **Brute Force** = This type of attack occurs when a number of randomly selected numbers, usernames, passwords and phrases are attempted to access a computer or network resource. The process is totally "Trial and Error". Either an actual person can physically attempt a brute force attack or software can be used to attempt thousands of random combinations.

- **Dictionary Attack** = This type of attack requires the use of some type of database of specific numbers, usernames, passwords and phrases. The elements have some form of association as well as a specific order of which combinations will be use first and last. The reason it is called a dictionary attack is due to the predetermined numbers, usernames, passwords and phrases selection much like that which appears in a dictionary.

- **Social Engineering** = Social engineering is the art of manipulating people and uses human interaction in order to derive confidential information. Using everyday seemingly normal conversations, the attacker is attempting to gain information such as passwords, confidential data locations or information on the physical location of servers or even information about what security measures are used in a company, business or organization. Social engineering involves face-to-face, telephone or other verbal communications

- **Baiting** = Making convenient access to a device such as a flash drive to a computer user who the "Bad Guy" wants to compromise. The person who picks up the flashdrive and uses it does not know that the flashdrive has software on it which will compromise the computer in various ways such as automatically installing monitoring or remote access software.
- **Phishing** = This occurs via telephone, e-mail and text messaging. Essentially, a message is received informing of some important occurrence (Lottery Winner, Bank Account Confirmation, System Update). Somewhere in the communication, there will be a request to send the message sender some type of confidential data (i.e., Username, Password, Account Number, etc.). Once the data is sent, the attacker now has the ability to either steal data or launch attacks against the user's servers.

Security Methods for Computers and User Accounts:

Although there is no perfect method of protecting data, computers, server and networks, there are a number of "best practices". These are methods advocated by computer professionals in areas of cyber-security based upon experiments, trails and even studies of cyber-attacks. This list is not all-inclusive but serve as a starting point for security discussions.

- **User Account Control (UAC)** = The UAC stops users from making changes to a computer's operating system. Remember, there are many different "User Types" on a windows computer. By default, only users in the group entitled "Administrators" can make operating system changes. When a program or a user not in the "Administrators" group attempts to make an operating system change, the UAC dialog box" appears requesting the credentials of an administrator. If the credentials are not those of an administrator, the UAC stops the installation of the program or the change to the operating system.
- **Trusted Platform Module (TPM)** = This is a security feature that has been developed and increasingly implemented over the last few years on for laptops and desktops. The system requires inter-related microchip circuitry which is part of the motherboard, BIOS and hard drive to provide hardware specific security. TPM has the ability to provide better confidentiality of data as well as storage of security

elements such as passwords, certificates and encryption keys. These elements allow security and confidentiality when accessing the computer or when the computer is being used to access online resource such as websites or gateway servers.

- **BitLocker** = BitLocker is a protection method which performs manipulation of the data on a hard drive via changing the order and arrangement of "bits" in messages and documents. At the time of this writing, BitLocker had the ability to utilize either 128 bit or 256 bit encryption. In addition to encrypting the data on a hard drive, BitLocker also protects the physical hard drive from being accessed by any operating system other than the one which originally communicated with the hard drive. The hard drive is also "married" to the motherboard to which the hard drive is originally connected to so if the hard drive is removed from the computer and replaced in a different system, the drive will be unusable. Because BitLocker requires a connection to both the original operating system and motherboard, many users become concerned that their data would be lost if the motherboard or any element outside of the hard drive were to fail. In the event that a system recovery is required, BitLocker also allows the creation of a "Recovery Key" which can be used to unlock the hard drive for maintenance or data recovery purposes.

- **Strong Passwords** = A method often utilized in basic level security of a user account or computer is via using an account which combines a "username (Collection of letters which represent a person, i.e., a person named "Bill White" might have a username of "BWhite")" and a password (A combination of keyboard characters known only by a particular user). It was thought at one time that the more characters you have in a password, the more secure it is. After much studies, it was found out that by combining the various characters available on a keyboard actually increases levels of security. Following that philosophy, Microsoft released recommendations for using what is called a "strong password". This type of password includes the following elements.
  - o 8 or more characters
  - o Random letters and numbers (Not in typical order such as "ABC", "123" or "QWE".
  - o Both Uppercase and Lowercase Letters
  - o Utilizing symbols when possible (Such as #, *, &, @, etc.).

- **Firewall** = A firewall is actually a very generic term. Traditionally, it describes a software or device which monitors access to a computer. Essentially, the firewall will look for activity which falls outside of a "baseline" (Standard for normal computer activity). When an activity outside of the baseline occurs, the firewall can automatically disconnect the connection or inform a computer user of the activity. As a comparison, think of a computer as a very popular "nightclub" with a dress code requiring a tie for males. At the door of the club, there are staff members who assure all males have ties. If a male attempts to enter without a tie, this would be "outside of the baseline" which will either cause the club staff to reject the male or ask management if the eager club goer should be allowed to enter.
- **Encryption** = This is the process of protecting data from being viewed by those other than the persons for which the data is intended. There are multiple types of encryptions but most are related to the base unit of data for computers defined as a "bit ("0" or a "1")". All computer data and communications are a collection of bits known as "binary numbers" (Such as the collection "00000011" which is the binary code for the decimal number "3" or "10000010" which is the binary code for the decimal number "130"). When encryption is involved, the arrangement of bits will be "scrambled" or "altered" in some way. In addition, some encryption software inserts "nonsense characters" which cannot be converted to anything. Encryption software might change the arrangement of bits to produce a different number. When this occurs, essentially there is a "locking" process which changes the bits, and a "Key" process which returns the collection of bits to their original format. Let's simulate an "Eight-Bit Encryption" process for the number "130" as an example:
    - **Step #1 (Locking process called "Encryption")** = Change every 8 bits of a message into the reverse of the bit which exists in the message. The message changes from "10000010" to "01111101" which is a totally different number (If you are curious, it is "125").
    - **Step #2 (Transmission process)** = Message is sent to recipient via available transport method (i.e., FTP, E-Mail, Text, etc.).
    - **Step #3 (Receiver uses Key (Called "Decryption")** = Decryption key Change every 8 bits of a received message into the reverse of the bit which now appears. The message changes from "01111101" back to the original "10000010".

- **Windows Security Policies** = Policies are what Windows uses to control items such as passwords, systems, permissions as well as tracking specific events. All versions of Windows do not have exactly the same security policies but they can appear in many different formats such as the following:
    - **Local Policies** = Only effects that specific computer.
    - **Domain Polices** = Affect all computers that are part of a specific network.
    - **User Policies** = Only affects persons logging into systems.
    - **Computer Policies** = Affect computers on a specific network.
    - **Group Policies** = Affects specific collections of users or computer accounts on either a single computer or an entire network.

There are a number of ways Windows security policies can be viewed such as using either "SecPol.msc" or "GPedit.msc" which would display the following:

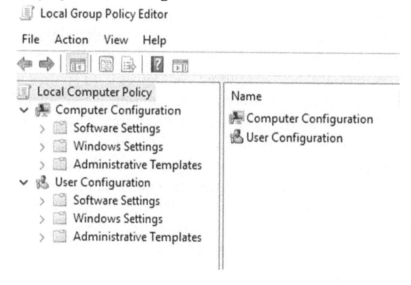

Within this policy you notice a number of options which can be configured. For example, if we wanted to manipulate password rules we could start from "Computer Configuration" all the way down through "Password Policies" in which we could define how many characters are required, how long the password can exist as well as if the password can be repeated are not.

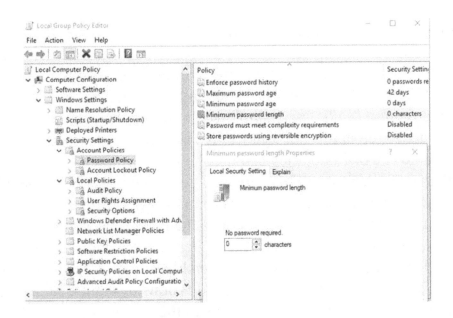

FAT32 vs. NTFS Comparison:

- **FAT32 Characteristics:**
    - Supports drive sizes up to only about 32 Gigabytes (Without special utility software).
    - Uses "Share" permissions to protect files from network access but any users who directly sits at and logs into the computer can access any folder within it.
    - Very compatible with a number of Windows and non-Windows operating systems.
    - The maximum size of a file or program can be only up to 4 Gigabytes in size.
    - Support for a name of a file is 8 characters (Plus "3" more normally reserved for type of file including spaces).
- **NTFS (New Technology Files System) Characteristics:**
    - Protects both the local system as well as network access to folders.
    - Support for a name of a file is 255 characters (Including spaces).
    - The maximum size of a file or program can be up to 16 Terabytes.
    - Has various types of "Permissions" and "Access Rights" which can limit the use and availability of files depending on the particular user attempting access the file, folder or program.

- **"Permissions" and "Access Rights"** = In the simplest terms, "Access Rights" are the users allowed to interact with a file or folder while "Permissions" are what the user will be able to do with a file or folder. When a file or folder is created by a user they automatically have the right of "Full Ownership" which means they can do anything they desire to the item. If a user desires another person to have access to the same file or folder they can use the items property sheet and add that particular user. There are also permissions such as "Deny" which prohibit a particular user (or group of users) from accessing an item. In fact, the "Deny" permission is the most powerful because it overrules any other permissions for an item. For example, you have a user called "Dude1" who has full ownership of a folder called "Dude1 Stuff". You can display the NTFS permissions by right-clicking the folder and bringing up its properties as in the following:

After displaying the properties it is possible to give any user permissions to the folder by clicking the "Edit" and "Add" buttons as in the following illustration:

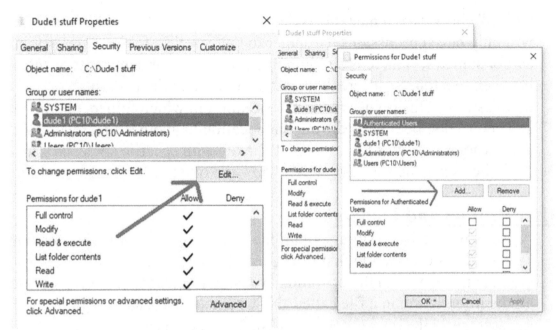

But say for example we place a folder inside of the "Dude1 Stuff" folder with a "deny" permission specifically for another user? Although we might have added a new user to the "Dude1 Stuff" folder they would not have access to the folder within it.

Permissions and Directories:

When a file or folder is created it immediately gets its permissions from the user. Additionally, depending on where the item is created it will reflect permissions and rights related to its location within the operating system directory structure. The process of these received permissions is called "Inheritance". As the item is manipulated however the permissions may be modified are even erased. This is an occurrence which normally exists when a file or folder is either moved or copied. The following are some of the results which occur in NTFS when a folder is manipulated:

- **Move or Copy an item to different folder inside the original NTFS partition** = It retains its permissions.
- **Move or Copy an item to different NTFS partition** = It inherits the permissions of the destination folder.
- **Move or Copy an item from an NTFS partition to a Fat32 Partition** = All NTFS permissions are erased.

It is possible to block permissions and stop them from being inherited from the encompassing folder. One way to enable this is to uncheck the "Allow Inheritable Permissions From Parent To Propagate To This

Object" check box. Once this is done any items created within the folder will only have permissions particular to that specific folder. As mentioned earlier sometimes there is a requirement to a copy large number of folders between two totally different computers but retain their original permissions. This is customary in a situation in which folders on network servers need to be migrated from one location to another. To retain all the permissions a utility such as "XCOPY.exe" with specific switches which could be used (Such as "/X", "/H", "/O" and others).

User Profiles and Folders

A user's profile is the storage of all the settings particular to that account. The profile is created the first time a user logs into a computer. The login creates an area within the operating system particular to that user storing all the information in a file called "NTUser.dat" associated with the registry key "HKEY_CURRENT_USER". There is also a directory path of "C:\Users" in Windows 10 in which all of the user profiles are stored as displayed in the following graphic:

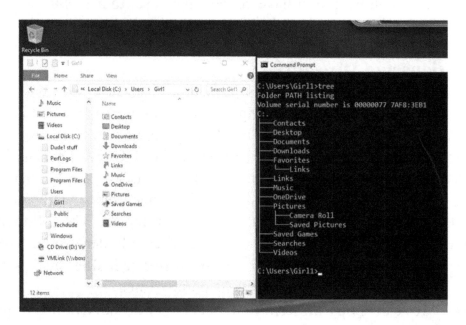

After successful login, a user can modify their profile to suit their activities. Profiles include some of the following elements:
- Desktop Picture and Theme.
- Size of Icons.
- Start Menu Options.
- Default Internet Browser.

Depending on the type of account, profiles can have the following definitions:

- **Local User Profiles** = All attributes in this profile are only stored on that particular computer.
- **Roaming User Profiles** = This type of profile is stored on a network server associated with multiple workstations. The profile will appear on any computer a particular user logs in on. In essence, the profile "follows" or "roams" to wherever computer the user is working on.
- **Mandatory User Profiles** = A standard profile created for all users in a company or business which cannot be changed by users. This is often done to assure all users have specific software or desktop arrangements related to that employees function.
- **Temporary User Profiles** = This appears when the profile associated with a particular user is unavailable because of some error. A blank profile appears upon the user's login which will not save any information for that user. When the user logs off any modifications of the profile are lost.

Chapter 9
Disaster Recovery Methods for Workstations

Computer Freezes, File Corruption and Crashes:

Although it will not occur every day (Hopefully), there is always the possibility of a computer failing. Server failure can have many definitions such as the following:

- Users cannot locate files on the network.
- The websites on internet are no longer accessible.
- Account login no longer works on any computer in the building.
- A computer screen appears "blank" or "black" with a blinking line in the upper-left corner.
- Users cannot find any of their e-mail.

There are thousands of reasons a system could stop operating such as hardware, software conflicts, virus, malicious attacks, and many more. Finding the reason for the failure, is a task for the future, however. The immediate task is to restore computers to normal functionality. If the employees of a company or business cannot access a network, they cannot work. Depending on the purpose of the business, money could be lost or functions can be hindered. It is very important that computer and business functionally be re-enabled as swiftly as possible. Not only for business continuity, but also for the computer technicians' job security. Understand, every hour longer it takes to fix the computer problem could bring the technician closer and closer to termination. In the end, it is always regarded as a technician's fault if anything remains damaged, regardless of the cause of the problem. Keeping the before mentioned in mind, it should always be a priority of the technology specialist (I believe it should be their 1st priority!) to have a method to move a computer back to functioning as quickly as possible. If the computer is working, less people will overwhelm the technician allowing him space and time to locate and eradicate the cause of the computer, server or network failure. Below are some of the options available which would allow the continued function of the system:

- **The Windows Registry** = This term is in reference to a database within the Windows Operating System. This database contains configuration, settings and preferences for the operating system, hardware and programs. Information included might be date of installation, licenses for access, expiration time for software with expiration periods, etc. On higher order operating systems (Server

2008, 2012, etc.) there are entries which control communications between servers and the internet. Be very careful, when accessing the registry. Modifications are instantaneous. An incorrect registry entry can totally disable a computer.

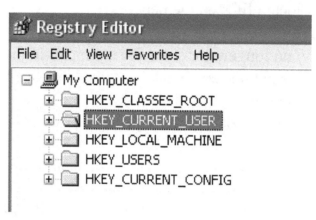

- **Task Manager** = In windows operating systems, the task manager is a utility which allows the monitoring and limited control of processes which a computer performs without user interaction. These processes are sometimes referred to as "Services" or "Functions". The ability for a computer to access the internet is a "service", how many times a program utilizes RAM for instructions might be classified as a "function". Using the task manager, it is possible to view how much RAM is being used, how busy the CPU is and how many users are remotely connected to a server. One of the most well-known functions of the task manager is the ability to cancel failed applications. In the event a program is "stuck" and stopping the use of other programs, the offending program can be terminated using the task manager freeing the user to continue to use other programs and the computer in general.
- **Event Viewer** = This MMC allows the viewing of application and operating system processes. It is possible to view occurrences of applications not loading or event tasks terminating incorrectly. The information is provided in different formats which allows critical evaluation of various processes. Within event viewer there are also comments associated with specific occurrences which can be used do diagnose various problems.

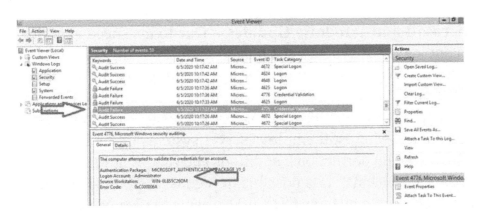

- **Performance Monitor** = This is like a "Dashboard" on the inside of a car. MMC allows viewing the conditions and status of various aspects of an operating system. There are a number of sections within Performance Monitor (Which can be launched with "Permon.exe" and "Perfmon.msc"). Counters include aspects of processes, resources, software and hardware. Some of the aspects include time use by the CPU for specific applications, total amount of RAM and current usage as well as the amount of time the hard drive is being used for specific processes. Depending on the counters selected, the resultant data can be presented in a number of graphic formats such as line graphs and column charts.

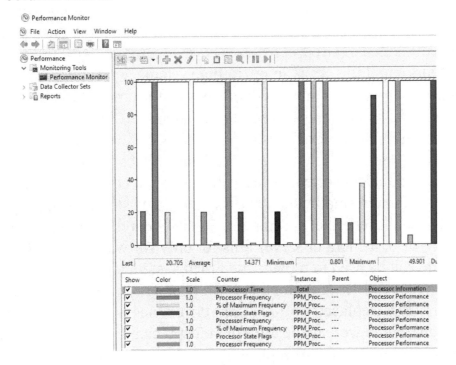

- **Microsoft and Windows Updates** = Due to the speed at which technology changes, there is a need to make changes in operating systems. In addition, often after an operating system is released, there is the potential for security flaws or conflicts between different files in an operating system. To control for failures to users, businesses and companies, Microsoft employs server systems throughout the world which contain corrections, additions and modifications to their operating systems. It is possible to request these modifications by e-mail (Or even mailed as CD/DVD's using the US Mail System) but Microsoft implemented a method which is somewhat automated as long as a computer has access to the internet. This process runs as a service called "Microsoft Updates". The service provides modification concerning Security and protections against malware, operating system bugs (features which have performance issues) and enhancements to tasks the operating systems can perform. According to many Microsoft documents, many updates are made available on the second Tuesday of each month (Many technicians refer to this day as "Patch Tuesday") computers will routinely check. If necessary computer technician can disable Microsoft updates and instead utilize "Windows Update". This is done by manually configuring a computer to access the Microsoft Update servers at a specific time to download a large file which will include Updates (Modifications to the Operating System), Patch's (Group of files used to repair a feature) or "Fixes (Repairs small file errors in operating system)."
- **Backup** = Process of making duplicates of files, programs and even completely functioning servers (Often called an "image"). It is important that these Backups are created at different times of the year (Such as "Monthly", "Once a Week", and "Once a Day") to reflect files which change often. These files are often compressed making them extremely small which allows them to be stored on flash drives, DVD's and even other computers. In the event the original files disappear or a client or server fails for only software causes, the backup can be used to replace the failed system and operations can continue. All files and functions will operate as if there had been no failure. The "replaced-original" servers or files will not include any changes which were made after the most recent backup.
- **Restore** = The process of replacing failed files, programs, clients or servers with fully-functioning versions which were previously created using some type of backup or imaging software. The "restored"

systems and files will operate normally allowing users to access files and perform functions which were supported by the original servers and files. In this scenario, there is a possibility that some data loss has occurred, but the loss is limited to a few days, versus a few years. The only missing items will be files which were created after the backup was created or programs installed after the image was created of the servers. These items can be re-installed or recreated.

- **Low Power States** = Often times when working on computers users take breaks or simply forget to turn the computer off at the end of the day. On a desktop which is connected to a power outlet it may not affect the overall operation of the system or the retention of files. On laptops and tablets which are battery powered, allowing the system to remain on can result in loss of data or the inability to use computer because the battery no longer has a charge. To combat this many operating systems have a "low-power" condition they can operate within in the event that a user has not interacted with the computer after a particular amount of time. The following are some of the types of low-power modes computers operate in when not being utilized:
  - **Sleep or Standby** = Supplies just enough power to the motherboard to temporarily store open documents and programs into RAM. The computer is still powered but the components such as the view screen, DVD drive and network interface no longer receive electricity. This mode is usually the quickest for a computer to recover from.
  - **Hibernation** = When a computer is in this mode its stores open documents and programs directly on the hard drive and no longer provides power to RAM. Recovering from this mode will normally take more time than if the computer was in sleep mode. This is a good selection if you know you will not be using your computer for a long amount of time.

Chapter 10
Installing or Upgrading an Operating System

Installing or Upgrading an Operating System:

In the computer field, there are a number of methods in which a Windows operating system can be installed. In order to begin the process of installing the operating system, a technician must get access to the "source files" for windows. The source files can come in some of the following forms:

- **DVD** = Optical Disc with all compressed binary files located on the disk.
- **ISO** = A file which is read as if it were a DVD.
- **Network Share** = Directory located on a server which holds expanded network binaries as full files in order to install the operating system.

After selecting the desired source file, there are a few methods of installation. These method options are available to customize the installation to either preserve present data or allow higher-order utilization operations. The following are some of the more well-known options:

- **Clean Install** = Totally erases all previous data on the computer. Existing directories, programs and files are essentially eliminated. This is normally the process when installing Windows on a brand new or "just built" computer system.
- **Upgrade** = This method allows migration from an older operating system to a newer operating system. An example would be moving from "Windows 7" to "Windows 10. When an "Upgrade" installation is done, the process attempts to preserve all previous data such as programs, directories and files. Be cautious with upgrades. All operating systems cannot be upgraded as well as some programs which work on older operating systems may not work on the most recent version of Windows. Always perform a complete backup of all essential programs and files and check the manufacturer websites for the programs and devices to assure the older products will operate on the upgraded version of Windows:
- **Dual Boot** = Often times there is a need to preserve a complete operating system while also utilizing an upgraded or different version. In addition, there might also be the need to have both operating systems access the same sets of unique files or directories. In this scenario, it is possible to install two (Or more) operating systems on the same computer. Literally, a computer can have

access to both "Windows XP" and "Windows 10". Or Windows and Linux or the MAC OS). When the computer has more than two operating systems, it is often called "**Multi-boot**".

<u>Windows Directory Structure</u>

This section is an attempt to better explain how operating systems store files. Most people who use computers depend on programs and applications to find documents they've created (Such as "Microsoft Word "Recents", Internet browser "History" or the "Search" option on the Start Menu"). As a computer technician it is important to have knowledge related to where files are located on a Windows system. The following are concepts related to the directory structure utilized in Windows and many other operating systems. When thinking about how an operating system stores files you should imagine a large "file cabinet" with many drawers. Each drawer in the cabinet contains folders. The folders have many pieces of paper, photos and other items. Inside of some folders, there are other folders also holding documents. Imagine that the person who owns the file cabinet is very organized and neat because they place a name tag on each drawer and folder to remember its contents. Within each drawer every folder is in alphabetical or numerical order. In addition, every paper within the folders are also in alphabetical or numerical order. And just to be extra cautious the owner of the file cabinet keeps a written list taped to the side of the cabinet so they know exactly what documents are within it and even when the documents were originally stored or changed. Take the

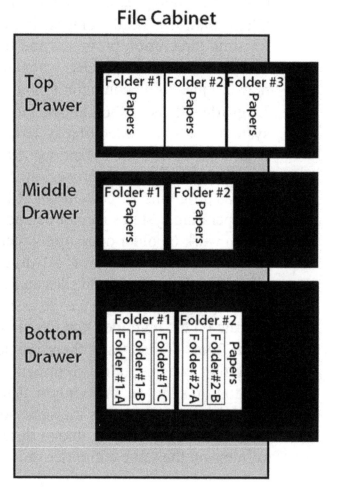

File Cabinet

following graphic as an example of a file cabinet:

When programmers design operating systems they use the same "file cabinet" concepts. Areas inside of the operating systems are created (Similar to "drawers" and "folders") within sections of memory (Either RAM or the hard drive) to store particular directories (Similar to "folders") and programs or files (Representing "papers"). To visualize this let's replace some of the names on the previous diagram with names normally related to computers.

The diagram to the right is a very simplified view of the directory structure which may exist within an operating system. Below is a more factual display of a directory structure. The first display is what many people are familiar with on a Windows Operating system using a graphical user interface (Also called "GUI"):

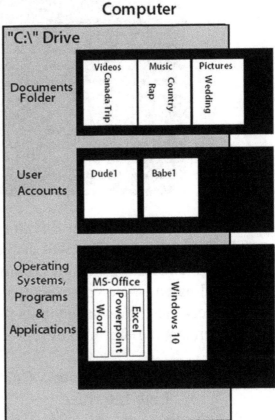

Directory Structure
Windows Graphical User Interface

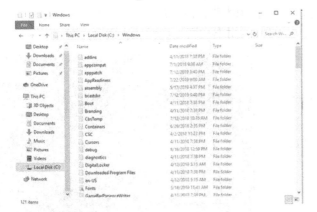

The next graphic displays the same information and location using a command line interface (Also called "CLI") after typing the command "DIR":

Directory Structure - Windows Command Line Interface

Another way to look at the directory structure relationship is by using the "TREE" command. This will display a logical diagram of directories as well as their relationships by connecting them with lines (Please Note: Depending on where you execute this command the readout can be extremely long. You can stop its process by holding down the "Ctrl" key and then tapping the "C" key):

Directory Structure - Windows Command Line Interface

All of the above are examples of how to view file locations in the Windows directory structure and some other operating systems. As a computer technician, it is essential to be able to imagine the location of files when attempting to either install or repair Windows computers. Experiment with the above functions, they cannot damage your system and will give you a better understanding of the Windows directory structure.

Copying and Moving Files:

When a computer is failing, it is essential to transfer as much data from the computer as possible as swiftly as possible. The different programs (i.e., Mozilla Firefox, Microsoft Word, Call of Duty, etc.) can be easily restored using purchased installation media. The documents which have been created for days, week, months or years have the most value. When the GUI fails on a computer, it is often required to perform a number of commands using the CLI. This is a valuable option in the event you can get the computer to boot up from a DVD, flashdrive on other manner which will allow command line control of the computer. After accessing the command line, it is possible to navigate to the directory (Also called "Folder") in order to copy any documents to an external drive or network location prior to attempting repairs on the failing computer. The following are two commands which are extremely helpful in copying large amounts of data from one location to another:

- **COPY** = This utility allows the duplication of files in a different location. There are a number of modifications which can be used with this command such as the following:
  - **Copy *.* E:\SaveDocs** = Copy all files to a folder called "SaveDocs" on a drive listed as "E:\" drive.
  - **Copy filename.ext E:\SaveDocs** = Copy a specific file from the present location to a folder called "SaveDocs" on a drive called "E:\".
- **XCOPY** = This utility allows the duplication of files folders and subfolders in a different location. There are a number of modifications which can be used with this command such as the following:
  - **xcopy c:\old *.* E: /s** = Copy all files, folders and subfolders to a drive listed as "E:\" drive. Errors in any particular file will stop the process of any remaining copies after the point of error.
  - **xcopy c:\old *.* E: /c** = Copy all files, folders and subfolders to a drive listed as "E:\" drive ignoring any errors which might occur with the copying of any particular file or folder.
- **ROBOCOPY** = This utility is a higher version of XCOPY implemented after Windows Vista adding more error correction, logs and other features. There are a number of modifications which can be used with this command such as the following:

- **robocopy c:\old *.* E: /E** = Copy all files, folders and subfolders to a drive listed as "E:\" drive. This also includes any empty subfolders.
- **robocopy c:\old *.* E: /S** = Copy all files, folders and subfolders to a drive listed as "E:\" drive excluding any subfolders which are empty.

Open a CLI on your system and attempt the above commands. None of the commands listed above will damage a computer. In addition, there are some exercises you can do using CLI which might assist in repairing or servicing a computer or network device in the future.

Replacing a Computer and Migrating Files:

Oftentimes, a technician must replace a failing computer. This is a project which will include a multitude of tasks. In addition, there are a range of options available concerning replacing a computer. If the failed computer has no important data, the process is somewhat easy. If there is data which must be preserved, however, the task then becomes somewhat complex. The data could be as simple as a picture of a loved one, or as important as the documentation of the proper sequence to administer medication. In any case, it is important to safeguard the information from loss in the event the computer totally fails so it can be utilized on the new computer. In order to protect data during installations, the following are some options which could be utilized:

- **File backup** = This is the process of making copies of different files and depositing them on some type of media. The media could be one of the following:
  - Flashdrive or Mobile Hard drive.
  - Rewritable DVD
  - Network Share
- **Application Backup** = In some operating systems, it is possible to make compressed copies of working programs on a computer. When this type of backup is completed, there is no need for the original installation media. It is possible to create files which will perform all of the operations of the installation media and those files can be stored either on the original computer or some other outside media.
- **Windows System Restore** = Within the Windows Operating system, it is possible to make a "compressed duplicate" of the entire

computer. The compressed duplicate appears as a "file" which can be stored on any file backup location. This is often referred to as a "System Restore Point". In the event that the computer was to fail, the existing computer can be totally erased and replaced with a fully functional version of the same computer which was created at an earlier date.

- **Windows Imaging** = After months of using a computer, a user develops a lot of documents, customizations and alterations to the actual computer itself. With so many modifications and documents on the computer, it is very important to make a backup of not only the documents on the computer, but the entire computer itself. There are many programs available to clone computers such as "Symantec Ghost", "Fog", "Clonezilla" and many others. In the field of computer technology, the process making a backup of a computer includes the following terms and definitions:
  - o **Image** = Name of a file which is a compressed copy of the entire computer.
    - ➤ This can also be called a "**recovery image**".
  - o **Cloning** = Process of making a copy of an entire computer.
  - o **Restore** = Process of installing an image on a computer (The same computer or a different system).
  - o It is also possible to create a backup of an entire Windows 10 computer without purchasing any other software. There are at least two methods to perform imaging in Windows:
    - ➤ **System Restore** = This is a GUI-based wizard within windows which allows a user with little or no computer technology experience to make a backup of an entire computer. It also allows the restore of the computer to a specific condition developed at a past date.
    - ➤ **RECIMG** = Command Line utility which requires firm knowledge of typing in specific commands in the CLI. The following command would make a complete backup of the computer and store the image file on an external drive with the name "BKWedJan1:
      - **Example** = "recimg /createimage f:\BKWedJan1"

Computer Malfunctions and Advanced Boot Options:

Addressing computer failures is a very time-consuming requirement when working as a computer technician. There is no perfect book" which will be able to list all the specific causes for a computer to malfunction. In most cases, there are multiple reasons which could be working in unison to cause a system to error. Three frequently occurring causes of failure are the following:

- **Changed screen Resolution** = Often a user experiments with the size of the icons on the monitor accidently changes the communication rate of light between the Video card and the monitor. This results in the screen display being extremely unclear or often times blank.
  - **Software installation** = Different programs will attempt to control the video card or the resolution of a monitor resulting in incorrect settings between the video card and the monitor.
  - **GUI failure** = The operating system files which control the graphical user interface are damaged, the screen will not display any icons although the computer is completely turned on.

When either of the above errors occurs, there is an option for repair called "Advanced Boot Options". This method allows the starting of the computer in the following states:

- **Safe Mode** = This allows the basic video settings to be applied. Any modifications attempted by resolution changes or software will be ignored. After booting in this manner, any resolution changes could be set back to standard windows settings (Often called "Default") or added software can be uninstalled. After making modifications, the computer can be restarted in normal mode and the errors are now eliminated.
- **Safe Mode with Command Prompt** = This mode allows the CLI of the operating system to start with no graphics. This mode is normally used when it is confirmed that the GUI will no longer load and the priority is to copy the files to another location such as a flashdrive or other external device connected to the computer. It is also possible to boot into "Safe Mode with Networking" to allow the system to book either to a basic GUI or the CLI and also having

connections to network devices such as servers, printers or even the internet.

Depending on the operating system (Windows XP, Windows 7, and Windows 8 thru 10) there are a number of ways to get to the Advanced Boot Options. It would exceed the expectations of this book to list all of the instructions so it is advocated that research be performed by the technician working on a system of the appropriate method to use based upon the computer in question. Below are some examples of what the menu may look like:

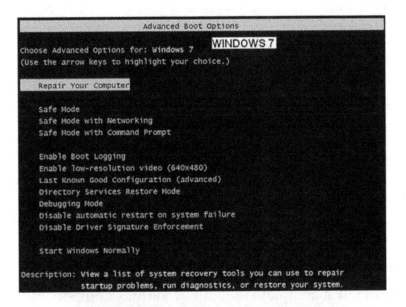

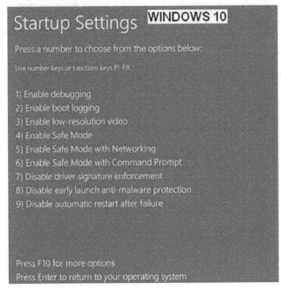

- **MSCONFIG**
  - There are many utilities which might be used to ascertain why a computer is experiencing errors. One such utility is "MSCONFIG". This utility controls what files, programs and commands the operating system will attempt to start when the computer is first turned on. It is possible to use the utility to customize how the computer will start. The following is a graphic display of MSCONFIG:

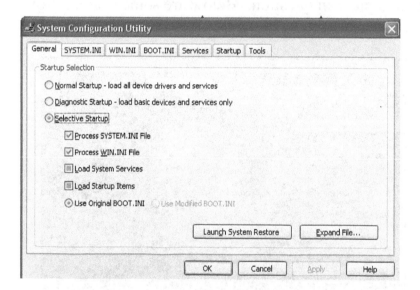

- **MSINFO32 (Often times just "MSINFO")** = This program allows a user to view a complete readout of various components in a computer system. Items displayed include RAM, Video Cards, Hard Drive, Device Drives and many other aspects of the system. This utility is often used by a technician to assure that the computer can support a device or software prior to installation. Below is a graphic of an MSINFO display:

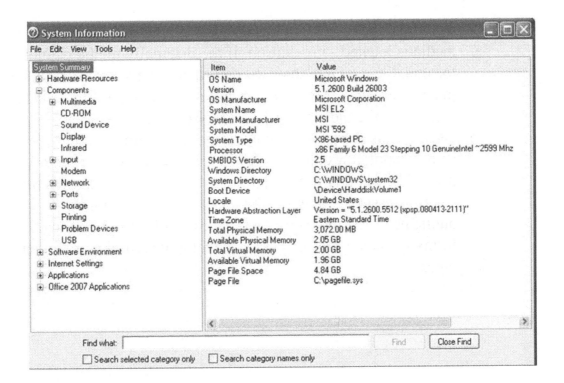

- **Windows Upgrade Assistant (Formally Called "Update Assistant")** = This utility facilitates moving lower operating system to a higher system (Such as "Windows 7" to "Windows 10"). In order to properly use this utility, the software is normally downloaded via "Windows Updates" or manually selected for download to a computer. After the program is started, it will assess capabilities of the computers CPU, RAM, etc. to ascertain if the hardware will support the new operating system. This is a very important tool to consider before attempting to "upgrade" an older system to a newer operating system. If an operating system is installed on a computer which cannot provide the RAM, drivers and CPU processing speed, the computer will not boot and all the data previously on the computer is lost.
- **System Protection** = Regardless of how careful a user is concerning operating a computer, there is always the potential of critical and fatal damaged. In order to safeguard programs and data, it is extremely important to always have a method to assure the continuity of two aspects of the computer system.
  - **Programs** = Applications installed on a computer which support specific user activities such as "Microsoft Word" for document creation and editing or "CakeWalk" which is a program for manipulating audio (Music) files. If these programs

were lost, the user often has no idea of where the installation media is located. In addition, if the originally media cannot be located, the user may have to repurchase the software or updated to a newer version of which might not be compatible with files created by the older versions of the software.

o **Data** = This is by far the most important element to be protected on a computer system. Each file is actually the creation of a user. The file might be a document which has thousands of pages of essential data. If the data is lost, it cannot be duplicated. Examples of these types of files might be legal forms, photos, programs under development and many other file types.

Chapter 11
Introduction to Network Technology

Introduction to Network Technology:

The "International Organization for Standardization" (Commonly called the "ISO") is an independent, non-governmental international organization based in Geneva, Switzerland. The participants of the ISO are considered to be experts who share knowledge and develop voluntary international standards to support innovation, consistency and global solutions to various worldwide situations. The members include over 161 national groups who all discuss, devise and develop standards for products, services and systems concerning quality and safety. There are over 21,000 International Standards and related ISO documents ranging from technology, food, energy, waste and many other areas. There are two primary models of communications in networking which are advocated by the ISO:

- **OSI Model (Open Systems Interconnect)** = A conceptual description listing the elements of network devices and how they communicate. This model separates network communication, software and devices into 7 distinct layers. Each layer supports specific functions, which in turn allow transition into layers either above or below it. Without going into detail, the following are the seven layers of the OSI model and some of the related features within each layer:

OPEN SOURCE INTERCONNECT (OSI-MODEL)				
LAYER#	NAME	FUNCTION	ASSOCIATION	PDU TYPE
7	APPLICATION	File transfer, e-mail	Browsers ms-outlook	DATA
6	PRESENTATION	Formats data for transfer	Ansi, oem, etc.	DATA
5	SESSION	Creates and coordinates connections between applications		DATA
4	TRANSPORT	Data flow and error correction	Tcp, udp	SEGMENT
3	NETWORK	Establishes communication path between nodes	Routers	PACKET
2	DATA	Conversion to bits	Switches	FRAME
1	PHYSICAL	Carries the bits	Hubs, nic's, cables	BIT
WAYS TO REMEMBER LAYERS ORDER (First letter of each word represents layer:				
ALL PIMPS SELECT THE NICE DIAMOND PIECES				
ALL PEOPLE SEEM TO NEED DATA PROCESSING				
PLEASE DO NOT THROW SAUSAGE PIZZA AWAY				

Internet Service Provider (ISP) Connection Options:

One aspect that all networks, large or small, have in common is that they must have some method to connect their devices to a large network such as the internet. The amount of traffic supported by the connection to the internet will vary greatly due to utilization of the network, available funds, location of building and many other elements. In all cases, all networks regardless of size will require a relationship with an Internet Service Provider (Often called "ISP"). The ISP is the direct connection between the user and the Department of Defense's internet backbone. In residential use, there are many connection types. Two well-known types would include "Cable" and DSL. The following paragraphs offer a brief overview of each technology.

- **Cable** = Television and Internet (And sometimes telephone land line) all use the same connection device to access the outside world. This type of connection is a "shared presence" for the neighborhood. All cable connections in a specific area are all routed to a single device called a "point of Presence (Also called "POP") and then routed to the company which provides the connection. The major disadvantages to this type of connection include the following:
  - **Security** = Although there are multiple protection features installed in this type of configuration, it is possible for more "talented" hackers to use this as a point to compromise the data of the other users in the area.
  - **Network Traffic (Often called "Broadcast Storm" or a "Bottleneck")** = Because all traffic travels thru the same device, it is possible for the communications from a neighborhood to get so crowded that all users connections become slow.
  - **Wire Installation** = With cable, a technician must go to the location and physically install wires throughout a home. This is sometimes costly because many rooms will require connections for phone, internet and television.
- **DSL (Digital Subscriber Line)** = This technology uses the normal phone lines which run directly from a telephone carrier to individual homes. This technology is primarily for the internet and phone. Television is not included. The following are some of the elements which must be considered when
  - **Pre-existing wires** = DSL requires land lines from existing telephones. Depending on the age and condition of those lines, an internet connection can fluctuate in its reliability.

Typical Devices on Networks:

In order to store and retrieve data, the internet requires the use network devices with many names. These devices hold and display movies, text, photos and many other products and services used in the world. The following are some of the terms affiliated with these network devices:

- **Client** = Computer-related devices which primarily access the data on servers. Examples of clients could include:
    - Personal home computer or a Smartphone.
    - Computers in a library or Cyber-Cafe.
    - Staff computers in a company.
- **Server** = In network technology, a "Server" is a system that "Gives out Stuff" or "Holds Stuff". There are many types of servers in operation such as the following:
    - Web servers which hold and display websites.
    - Video Servers which allow access to movies online.
    - Email servers for transmitting and receiving texts and documents.
    - Domain Name Servers which allow users to find internet websites using a friendly name.
- **Hubs** = This device is one of the oldest used in networks. This device essentially multiplies physical connections to a network. For example, if there is normally a single connection which leads to the internet in a building. The hub would allow multiple devices access to this single connection. The devices could be computers, printers, or even video cameras. We normally classify hubs as "legacy devices". A legacy device is something that is based upon older technology but is still often used today. When selecting to use a Hub on a network, there are a few "Pros" and "Cons" which should be considered:
    - **Pros:**
        - **Inexpensive** = Hubs are often sold for under $60 dollars for small home offices.
        - **Easy to use** = No configuration required. Simply plug in the ports and electricity and they operate.
        - **Widely available** = Due to the number of years they have been around, they can be found thru any network technology supplier.

o>**Cons:**
- ➤ **Divides bandwidth** = Each device you plug in will reduce the bandwidth the hub is rated to support. Take the following example:
  - ❖ A hub which operates at 10Mbps has 10 available ports.
    - ☐ If two devices are connected, the hub now runs at 5Mbps.
    - ☐ If ten devices are connected, the hub now runs at 1Mbps.
- ➤ **Requires close physical proximity for repair** = Traditionally, there is no way to access, maintain or repair a standard, base-model hub unless you can touch it. If a person's office is on the 4th floor of a building but the connection leads to the hub in the basement, someone will have to walk to the basement to address the hubs fault.
- ➤ **Single-port signal** = Essentially one unit of data can pass thru the hub at a given time (Please note that this is in "milliseconds"). While that single data unit passes thru a single port in the hub, no other transmissions can occur on the other ports.

- **Switches** = This device operates much like a hub except it compensates for some of the disadvantages associated with hubs. The prices for switches range from moderate to extremely expensive (Some models cost $8,000.00 or more). The following are some aspects concerning switches:
  - ➤ **Multiplies network connections** = One port is normally connected to the network while dozens of others are connected to other network devices (Hubs, Switches, etc.) or computer systems (Servers, clients, printers, phones, etc.).
  - ➤ **Dedicated bandwidth** = No bandwidth is divided due to connected devices. Regardless the number of physical connections, switches will maintain the bandwidth for which they are rated.
  - ➤ **Multiple lines of simultaneous communications** = Switches allow multiple signals or communications to travel thru the devices at essentially the same time.
  - ➤ **Remote access** = A switch can be configured to allow connections from anywhere in the world as long as it has an IP

address and electricity being supplied. There are multiple methods of "remote access" utilized on switches and other network devices.

> **Network Segmentation** = Mid-range and higher switches have the ability to separate and segregate section of a network. This process is called "VLANs (Virtual Local Area Networks)". Some VLAN implementations are for the following:
>> **Security** = Assuring specific groups of computers cannot interact with other computers (i.e., student computers versus teacher computers).
>> **Bandwidth conservation** = A single computer uploading or downloading large files can hamper a network. If you segment the network with VLANs, only computers on that particular VLAN would be hampered. Operations on the other computers would occur because they do not know the other VLANs exist.

- **Routers** = These network devices are the primary connection points of the internet. Essentially, each building which has an internet connection normally has all of the switches connected in series terminating into a Router. The router provides the connection to an Internet Service Provider (ISP) which is connected to the internet backbone (Really the Department of Defense for whichever country you presently reside). In addition to the primary internet connection, Routers also provide the following functions:
  > **Remote access** = A Router can be configured to allow connections from anywhere in the world as long as it has an IP address and electricity being supplied. There are multiple methods of "remote access" utilized on routers and other network devices.
  > **Filtering** = Signals on the internet constantly travel and will attempt to flow into networks for which they are not destined. Routers will block any communications which attempt to access a network in which the desired target does not exist.
  > **Traffic Flow** = The internet is a large, complicated set of interconnected pathways. Routers can learn the fastest routes between sending and receiving devices. In addition, when a pathway fails, routers have the ability to negotiate with other routing devices to find other ways to destinations. Routers are often regarded as the "Traffic Cops" of the internet.

Signals, Cables and Connections:

All network devices are connected in some format. The actual connections are all over the world. Sometimes deep underground, some undersea and others going well above the earth to return to a remote destination. The various network connections use metal wires, "glass-like" fibers while others can communicate through the air without being physically connected. In conversations concerning network technology another way of saying "connection type" is "media" or "medium". Various media have different types of signals, connectors, lengths, advantages and disadvantages. The following are some of the media used in various types of networks.

- **Network Interface Card (NIC)** = This term often describes the internal portion on a computer which controls connections to a network through the use of some type of connection media which could be metal, fiber or wireless.
- **Port** = This term describes the connection point into a NIC or interface on switch or router.
- **Coax** = (Short for "Coaxial Cable") is one of the oldest network technology media. This cable has been used since the late 60's. More recently Coax is used primarily in visual implementations such as CCTV (Closed Circuit Television). A version of it is also used by some cable television carriers to connect a home modem or "Home Router" to the demarc in the house (The hole in the wall which connects to your ISP (Internet Service Provider). Coax comes in the two following versions:
  - ➤ **ThickNet** = Cabling of this type is older and not used frequently. It can be found connecting older buildings within corporate complexes, libraries or universities. ThickNet is about 1/2 inch in diameter and one of its major disadvantages was that it was not very flexible. The primary transmission speed most ThickNet networks achieved was up to 10 Mbps with a maximum single length of no more than 500 meters (Approximately 1,640 feet). ThickNet is often referred to as 10Base5 (The maximum distance of a segment equals 500 meters, so it was agreed upon to drop the last two zeros).
  - ➤ **ThinNet** = ThinNet resembles the type of wire which is often used to connect home subscriber's television to cable boxes TV. ThinNet coax is about 1/4 inch in diameter and is more flexible

then ThickNet. The longest span of a ThinNet cable is 185 meters (607 ft.). When describing this cable, it is often referred to as 10Base2 (Persons in the field desired to "abbreviate" the name for the technology. Since the maximum distance is 185 meters, it was agreed upon to "round the 185 up" to "200" and then drop the two zeros). This type of network media uses a connector called a "BNC (British Navel Connector).

- **Category Cable (Also called Twisted Pair or "Cat")** = Cable of this type is what we often see connected to telephones or basic network devices. The normal distance limitation of category cable is about 100 meters (Approximately 328 feet). The other name. "twisted-pair" originates from the construction of the cable. Within the cable, there are multiple-pairs of wires which are twisted in parallel (Side-by-side).

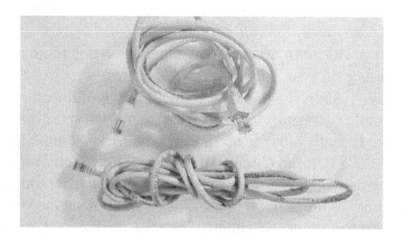

- There are many definitions concerning twisted pair cabling. One definition is based on the material used in the cable creation. Below appear the three primary material types:
  - ➤ **Shielded Twisted Pair (STP)** = Metallic foil surrounds the twisted wire pairs within the cable. The foil increases protection against electromagnetic interference which allows for faster data transmissions. STP is sometimes more expensive due to its composition and devices which might be required to provide better protection against EMI such as termination and grounding.
  - ➤ **Unshielded Twisted (UTP)** = Cable of this type has layer of material specifically provided for protection. It is often the type of cable viewed directly connected to computers from a hub or a switch.

- ➤ **Plenum-Rated** = This type of cable incorporates special materials in the cable covering. The makeup of the cable includes flame-retardant synthetics and low smoke materials to provide increased resistance against fire or the emission of toxic gasses.
- **Category Cable Specifications** = Different versions of category cable have numbers which indicate their use. Below are some of the category types:
  - ➤ **Cat-1 thru 3** = Primarily telephones and older basic technology.
  - ➤ **Cat-4** = Supported speeds of 16 Mbps
  - ➤ **Cat-5** = Supports speeds of between 10/100 Mbps (Called "FastEthernet).
  - ➤ **Cat-5e** = Supports speeds of 1000 Mbps speeds (Called Gigabit Ethernet)
  - ➤ **Cat-6** = It's suitable for up to 10 gigabit Ethernet (Called "10GigE) and has an internal separator between pairs of wires to protect from signal crosstalk (Signals from one set of wires interfering with signals on other wires).

- **Terminators and Connectors:**
  - ➤ **RJ-45 (Registered Jack #45)** = Network cable device connector. Notice that it has a "Clip" on it to secure it into network ports. Also, these terminators have a total of 8 individual wires which are secured into the terminator by metallic "pins" which dig into each wire to conduct electricity.

  - ➤ **RJ-11 (Registered Jack #11)** = Primary connector with telephones (Looks just like the RJ-45 except it only has about 4 pins).

- **Wire Specifications for Category** = Cables have individual wires in a particular arrangement within the RJ-45 connector as specified by

Telecommunications Industry Association (TIA). These arrangements of wires allow specific communications between network devices and have particular names such as 568A and 568B as illustrated below. Notice that the primary difference from 568A is the wires placed in Pins 1, 2 and 6:

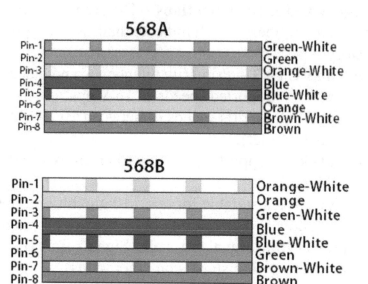

- **Terms for Cables with Specific Wiring Arrangements =** Depending on what the cable is connecting will dictate the wiring arrangement which also has a term to describe the cable. The following are often used cables in network technology:
  - **Straight-Cable** = This cable has both ends configured with one wiring scheme (Either 568A or 568B). This is a type of category cable which is used to connect dissimilar devices in the following manner.
    - Computer to Hub or Switch
    - Switch to Router
  - **Crossover Cable** = This cable has each end configured with one a different wiring scheme (568A on one end and 568B on the other). This cable is used to connect similar devices such as in the following:
    - Switch to Switch
    - Router to Router
    - Computer to Router (Not very frequently but can be done)

➢ **Rolled Cable** = This cable traditionally has a 568A standard but it is reversed on one end of the cable (Exact opposite on both ends). Also, this cable is normally "flat" and might be "light-blue" or "black" in color. Rolled cables are used for "Configuration" of devices and not network "Communications". Also, this cable normally has an "adaptor" on it so it can be connected to a "serial" interface on a computer.

• **Fiber-Optic Cable** = This media is comprised of an almost hair thin material referred to as "Glass" which is encased in mirrored cladding and a protective outer sleeve. Essentially, signals of light travel thru fiber allowing incredibly fast speeds (Upwards of 10,000 Mbps). It also allows communications over long distances (2 kilometers and greater). Due to its construction fiber-optic cable is very expensive. Although there are many type of fiber-optic cable, two will receive attention in this text:
  ➢ **Multi-mode** = 550 meters
  ➢ **Single-Mode** = support runs between 2 meters and 10,000 meters
• Connector types for fiber cable vary in construction. Some types which might be found on a fiber-based network include the following:

Straight Tip Connector (ST)   **Standard Connector (SC)**

Lucent Connector (LC)   **Small Form Factor Pluggable (SFP)**

- **Bandwidth** = This term describes the maximum amount of data which can exist on a connection at the same time. Contemporary network devices operate at one of four speeds: 10, 100, 1000 or 10,000 Mbps. If devices of different speeds are directly connected the "faster" port will reduce its speed to match the speed of the "slower" port. Please note, although the speeds are very distinct, an active connection only uses a portion of the available port speed. Think of it as a garden hose which has a "trickle" of water passing thru it at one time while other times the faucet is fully turned on and the entire inside of the hose is filled with water traveling towards the spout.

- **"Amounts", "Units" and "Speeds" in networks** = There are many descriptions which attempts to define maximum amount of data with the longest time it takes for a message unit to travel from a source to a destination. This is specified by the type of technology the message is using to travel. There are various types of networks technology, each with specific distance advantages and limitations. In this book, we include discussions which reflect the following speed format:
  - **bps** = Bits per second.
  - **Kbps** = Kilobits per second (Equal to 1000 bps).
  - **Mbps** = Megabits per second (Equal to 1000 kbps).
  - **Gbps** = Gigabits per second (Equal to 1000 Mbps).

- **Wireless** = Wireless networks exist between nodes which use the "air" as a medium. Clients transmit and receive either "light/sound/or radio" waives for communication. Some popular wireless technologies are the following:
  - **Bluetooth** = Very popular connection technologies used in cars, cell phones, entertainment systems, etc. Bluetooth requires very little equipment and operates on very low power. The range for Bluetooth networks varies from 33 feet to 10 meters depending on the class device in use.
  - **NFC (Near Field Communication)** = NFC allows devices such as a smartphones, printers and computers to communicate. The primary limitation of NFC is the range. Basic NFC requires the devices to be within about 2 inches of each other for communication. This type of technology is often used to allow two cell phones to transmit data between them if they are held close together.

➢ **802.11 Standards** = These are documents which discuss and illustrate recommended methods of wireless communications which were created by the Institute of Electrical and Electronics Engineers (IEEE) LAN/MAN Standards Committee (Also called "IEEE 802"). There are a number of versions of the "802.11" many of which began in the mid-1990's. Some of the more better-known standards include the following:

Standard	Frequency	Maximum Throughput	Distance (Radius)
802.11a	5 GHz	54 Mbit/s	115 feet (Obstruction limited)
802.11b	2.4 GHz	11 Mbit/s	115 feet
802.11g	2.4 GHz	54 Mbit/s	125 feet
802.11n	5GHz and/or 2.4GHz	300 Mbit/s	230 feet (Obstruction limited)

Network Topologies:

This term identifies the anticipated design or the existing arrangement of devices on a network. Servers, cables, rooms, routers, switches and many other devices can be included in the layout of the network topology. Often times, different parts of the network may be evaluated in a manner which requires only specific elements of the network to be displayed. When this occurs, a subset of a topology is created called a "Network Decomposition" which filters out anything extraneous to the aspects of the network elements under evaluation. At the root levels, there are two essential levels of a network topology. Those would be the "Logical" topology and the "Physical" topology.

- **Logical** = This network decomposition lists the identities of network devices in groups. Presently, an accepted standard is to utilize the IP addresses of nodes and hosts in reference to their associations and establishing which part of the network in which the device resides. Additional descriptions and symbols identifying items such as firewalls, e-mail servers and domain controllers often accompany many of the characteristics of a Logical Topology. Below are some examples:

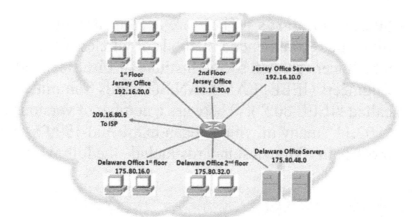

Company WAN example

- **Physical** = This network composition identities how devices are physically connected to one another based on cables, wireless and other connection media. There are characteristics of actual distance and proximity of devices. In addition, the arrangement of media connections are also highlighted on physical topologies which results in various names for specific designs. Below are some examples of Physical Topologies:
  - ➢ **LAN (Local Area Network)** = Network which includes communication connected computers within close proximity of one another such as a room or building.

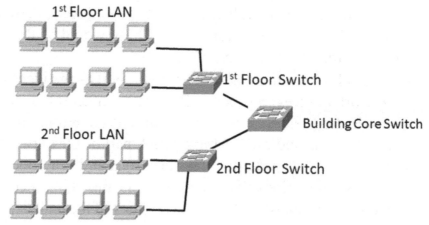

  - ➢ **MAN (Metropolitan (or "Medium") Area Network)** = Collection of connected LANS spanning the territory of a complex, campus or city.
  - ➢ **WAN (Wide Area Network)** = This network is a collection of connected MANS which are separated by large geographic

distances such as in state to state or country to country. One of the best examples of a WAN is the internet.

➢ **BUS** = Network setup in which each computer and network device are connected to a single cable or backbone. This topology was the standard during the beginning of most company and building networks. The primary disadvantage to a bus network was in the fact that if a single break was on the line, all network communication would cease.

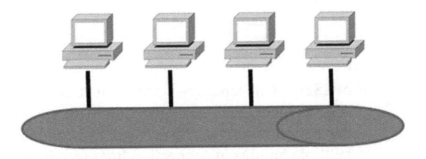

➢ **RING** = A circular design for a network in which a PDU travels from one node to the next in a specific sequence. In the early implementations of this topology, the PDU only traveled in a single direction. If there was a single break in the line, all communications would stop.

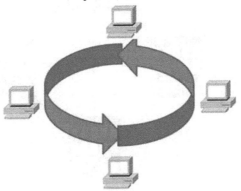

➢ **STAR** = Using a "Central Point" for communications, all nodes are connected via the central point which is often a hub or a switch. The PDU travels independently of the number of nodes and the failure of any node will not disrupt the others. The single disadvantage in this typology is that the central point is very critical if it fails, the entire network will not operate.

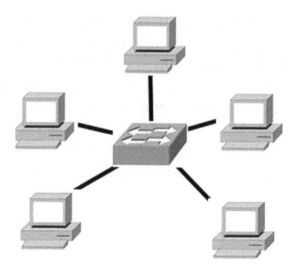

> **MESH** = This topology is the most stable. Essentially, every node as more than one connection to all the other nodes. Using this connection style, the network can continue operating with multiple failures in connection lines or nodes. The primary disadvantage to this topology is the redundancy increases the cost of the network due to the duplicated lines and devices.

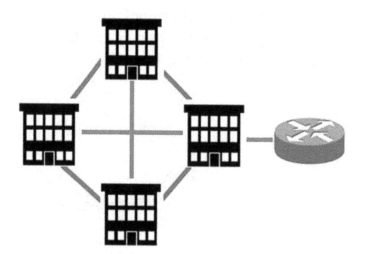

Internet Protocols (Network Language for Communications):

Regardless of the type of computer, there must be software to allow it to be managed and to allow it to communicate. The software for computer communications is referred to as a "Protocol" (Best definition is simply an "Agreed method of communication"). The names of some of these protocols are often used to describe what makes up the primary communication standard for computers on both small business networks and networks as large as the Internet. The following protocols and terms are highlights of software which allows computers to communicate:

- **HTTP (Hypertext Transfer Protocol)** = This allows network devices to display text, graphic images, sound, video, and other multimedia files on applications known as "Browsers" (i.e., Internet Explorer, Chrome, Safari, etc.).

- **HTTPS (Hypertext Transfer Protocol Secure also called "Secure Sockets")** = This is used for sensitive data and transactions such as billing, credit cards transactions, user login and many other processes where security of data is required. The protocol "scrambles" the data being transmitted so it is difficult to read if captured by some other device or person. In addition, it attempts to create a more dedicated private connection between a user's web browser and the web server. Often times, HTTPS can be combined with many other security options such as web or e-mail certifications.

- **FTP (File Transfer Protocol)** = This is used to move files between computers. This is what occurs in the background when photos or other files are posted to online services such as "Facebook" or "ITunes". This is a robust protocol which checks each "part" of a file to make sure the total file has no errors in transmission.

- **WWW (World Wide Web)** = The term "Internet" is now used synonymously with WWW but there is an essential difference. Think of the "Internet" as a "large book" with many pages and chapters. World Wide Web (or "WWW") is the "Table of Contents" used to locate the specific item in the book in which a person has interest in researching. This term describes a searchable information storage system which includes entries from all over the earth. The items in the information system could be as small as two or three sentences on a document to as large as books with thousands of pages. In addition to text-based information this global information resource includes videos, music, graphics and interactive systems used for both knowledge, education and entertainment. Some of the earliest implementations of the World Wide Web are attributed to the work of Tim Berners-Lee as recently as 1989. He compiled code which allowed access to the global bank of knowledge known as WWW via using code such as HTML (Hypertext Markup Language), URLs (Uniform Resource Locators) communication protocols such as HTTP (Hypertext Transfer Protocol) and internet browsers (Netscape Navigator, Internet Explorer, Mozilla Firefox and Google Chrome).

- **URL (Also called a "Uniform Resource Locator")** = This item is best referenced as "Whatever a person types in a browser to get to a website". Take "Facebook.com" for example. When a person desires to go to Facebook, those are the words they place in the top of most browsers (That area is called an "Address Bar".). The address "Facebook" is not a single server on the internet. It reflects dozens of servers owned by Facebook to provide their services. A "URL (Uniform Resource Locator)" has the same purpose as a UNC (Universal Naming Convention) in that it is used to locate a file or program stored on a network device. The primary difference is in that a URL normally references a resource on a network other than the network the user is located within. Traditionally, this "other network" is a different company or an item on a server located somewhere on the internet. Although the purpose of both UNC's and URL's are identical, the elements and characters in a URL are different. URL (Uniform Resource Locator) commands have what is often called a "Protocol Identifier" followed by a "Colon (:)." In addition, the "sections" in a URL are separated by the character often referred to as a "Forward slash (/)". Examples of Protocol Identifiers would be as follows:
    - **HTTP** = Hypertext Protocol (Website display and viewing).
    - **HTTPS** = Secure Hypertext Protocol (Protected internet transactions).
    - **FTP** = File Transfer Protocol (For upload and download of files).
- **FQDN (Fully Qualified Domain Name)** =This is the name of the server or group of servers which are registered with the internet. Each server or group of servers use a name followed by what is referred to as a "Top Level Domain (i.e., ".com", ".org", ".net", etc.)." Each server directly connected to the internet must be registered with a number of different organizations (i.e., Arpanet, Department of Defense, etc.). These organizations own DNS servers (Domain Name Servers) which are the "Table of Contents" or the "Phone Book" for the internet. Essentially, when anyone attempts to access a website, the request is first sent to a DNS server which looks for the name which had been typed in an address bar (i.e., "Google.com", "Facebook.com", etc.). The DNS servers respond by sending an IP address to the browser being used which allows the browser to locate the requested website. The syntax for a URL would be as follows:

- o **Protocol Identifyer://FQDN/DirectoryName/specific-file or Program such as the following:**
  - ➤ HTTP://Cooltoys.com/westcoast/trains.html
- o The following is a brief explanation of the syntax used:
  - ➤ **HTTP:** = Informs the operating system and browser what protocol is used for communication.
  - ➤ **"//"** = Instructs an operating system to access a network device listed on the internet as "Cooltoys.com".
  - ➤ **"/"** = Instructs an operating system to enter a directory called "westcoast".
  - ➤ **"/trains.html"** = Instructs an operating system and browser to display a web document entitled "Trains.html".
- **NetBIOS (Network Basic Input/Output System)** = This protocol which allows software on computers to exchange information a local area network (LAN). Client identities are identified using alpha-numeric identities (0-9 and A-Z). Often identities were limited to 8 characters or less.
- **NetBeui (NetBIOS Extended User Interface)** = This is an older protocol used for DOS and original Window networks (Primarily Windows 3.10 and Windows 95) designed for a single LAN segment. The protocol will not allow communications between discontinuous networks.
- **WINS (Windows Internet Name Service)** = This associates NetBIOS names to IP addresses on a LAN. This software was run as a service on a server to allow clients to locate other clients which might be on other LAN segments. WINS alone is non-routable but the software can be "carried" within another protocol such as networks that use NetBIOS over TCP/IP (NetBT).
- **IPX/SPX (Internet Packet Exchange/Sequential Packet Exchange)** = This is a LAN communication protocol developed by one of the original companies for network communications known as Novell networks. This protocol uses hexadecimal identities (0-9 and A-F) for devices and cannot be routed on the internet.
- **TCP/IP (Transmission Control Protocol/Internet Protocol)** = Method for communications between computers on small and large networks. The protocol is actually a combination TCP/IP is a combination of two protocols suites verbally separated for easier explanation. Each suite is a combination of protocols, but they have the same purposes as in the following:

- o **Transmission Control Protocol (TCP)** = Attempts to assure the dependable transmission of data between networks and devices. Within this capacity, the protocol will attempt to correct for data errors and requests re-transmissions of lost data.
  - o **Internet Protocol (IP)** = Attempts to define the path that data, signals, packets, pdu's, etc., will take to travel between a sending device and destination.
- **IPv4 (Internet Protocol Version 4)** = The primary protocol in data communication over different kinds of networks. This protocol identifies network devices by a 12-character decimal identity separated into 4 sections (192.168.1.1). Using this system allowed a worldwide network with over four billion IP addresses. With the increase of internet-connected devices (i.e., cell phones, car and home security, etc.) however, there is the potential of running out of IP's which can be accessed over the internet. Due to the address limitation, networks presently use other identity methods including IPv6, CIDR and VLSM (Terms will be explained and described later in this text).
- **IPv5 (Known as "Internet Streaming Protocol")** = This was primarily used for transmitting video and direct communication between routing devices for services for routing. Extremely fast and robust with multiple applications but requires high-end network devices for implementation.
- **IPv6 (Internet Protocol Version 6)** = This utilizes a combination of 32 hexadecimal characters for the identity of network devices. An example of an IPv6 identity would be "fe80::75ea:6ec0:e6f8:f037". This method allows close to 340 undecillion available IP addresses. IPv6 also understands communications from IPv4 devices. Unfortunately, IPv4 devices cannot understand communications directly from IPv6 networks unless there is a software or device in between the different networks to provide data conversion.
- **DHCP (Dynamic Host Configuration Protocol)** = This protocol gives identities to network devices in the form of an IPv4 address. The protocol will also provide network settings so network devices can find networks outside of the specific LAN. DHCP also attempts to assure that duplicated IP addresses are not given out to multiple network devices which could cause an entire network to stop functioning.

- **DNS (Domain Name System (or Service or Server))** = This associates domain names with IP addresses. Whenever someone wants to go to "Disney.com" the request goes to DNS servers around the world. Those servers have a "Shared list" which includes all known domains linked to IP addresses. Once the domain is found in the DNS server, the IP address is sent to the computer which requested the domain. The computer then uses that address to get to the desired domain.
- **Telnet** = This is a protocol which uses a "Command Line Interface" which allows connection to network devices (Routers, Switches, Computers, etc.) over vast TCP/IP distances. Options for use include browsing directors and limited "Text-based" control over devices. Although very effective, telnet is highly unsecure for PDU's are easily read with widely available software.
- **RDP (Remote Desktop Protocol)** = This allows a user to access a system without the need for being physically in the same location as the device. It is often used by various tech support services. Essentially, a person can sit anywhere in the world and interact with a computer as if they were setting directly in front of the computer. This protocol also enables a number of features of assistance to most computer or network devices interaction such as the following:
  - ➢ Mouse and keyboard
  - ➢ Data encryption
  - ➢ Audio, printer and file redirection
  - ➢ Clipboard sharing between a remote server and a local client

Chapter 12
Computer Network Utilities, Software and Commands

Computer Network Utilities, Software and Commands:

Working on networks often requires various tasks such as identification of devices, location of routes of travel and other elements common to communication networks. In our present day of technology, many operating systems and devices include applications and software-based tools to assist in computer assessment and troubleshooting. Many of these tools require the familiarization with the use of the "CLI (Command Line Interface)". The following are commands which prove very useful when interacting or repairing computers on a network:

- **Hostname** = This command appears in Microsoft Operating Systems and Cisco Devices. Depending on the platform, it can display the alpha-numeric identity of a system and/or change the identity of the system. The following are two of the utilizations of the command:
    - o Microsoft Server and Client platforms = Displays name of computer.
    - o Cisco Routers and Switches = Allows changing of a devices name.
- **IPCONFIG** = Displays basic required network settings on Microsoft platforms. The command also has an optional modification of the command which will show a complete display of communication configurations. In order to use the enhanced features, additional words and characters must be appended to the command. The character which must be added is often called a "Forward Slash" or a "switch". The character visually is represented by using "/".
    - o Available switches:
        - ➤ All = Displays interfaces, protocols and settings.
        - ➤ Release = Informs the DHCP server the client no longer requires an IP address.
        - ➤ Renew = Requests an IP address from a DHCP server.
- **Ping** = Assesses the ability of one computer to contact another computer. Often used to assess if a computer can reach a printer or someplace on the internet. Much like other command line utilities, there are options available to manipulate the data reported by the "ping" command such as the following switches:
    - o –t = Continually attempt to find target IP until "cancel" command is executed (Ctrl+C).
    - o –n (Count) = Set number of times to attempt to contact target IP.

Remote Access Services:

This is software which allows a person to literally view and control a computer system from a location physically removed from the actual computer. A person can be sitting in an office in Texas while controlling a computer in Pennsylvania. The person operating the computer is called a "Remote User". Every activity which can be performed while sitting directly in front of the computer can be done remotely. There are different categories of remote services as in the following:

- **Remote Assistance** = This is often used when a computer user is having difficulty with a program. What often occurs is that the user will contact "Help Desk" or "Tech Support" of some type. Often using an e-mail or a website, the user activates the connection. After the connection is made, the tech can see the screen of the computer user and give instructions on what the user must do to address the need at present. If necessary, the user can grant the technician the right to control the mouse and keyboard as well as record the session.

- **Remote Desktop** = This level of remote service allows the single user to use the computer as if they are at that location. They have full access to any programs on the computer as well as printers or any other devices locally connected to the computer. With this type of connection, the computer may or may not show that it is being operated remotely.

- **Terminal Application Services** = This method is used by companies, businesses and organizations to streamline computer programs and possibly reduce the cost of applications. Essentially, a single (Or sometimes two servers for redundancy) will have all the programs which are used by a company. All the users in the company have computers but there are no programs on them (This type of computer is often called a "Thin Client"). When the user requires a program, they use their local computer to access the "Terminal Application Server" which offers them the use of the program without installing the software on the computer. Documents created in this manner can be stored either on the server or the local computer. An attractive feature of Terminal Application Services is that when applications or programs must be updated or changed, the process occurs in one or two locations as opposed to servicing every computer on the network. A disadvantage to this method is often the cost of the server however because it must be very high powered to support multiple almost simultaneous connections daily.

Chapter 13
Identities and Character-Types

Identities and Character-Types:

Depending on which protocol or software is used on a network, devices can be identified many different ways. The following methods are ways in which network devices display their existence as well as what can be used for communications between devices (Note: Regardless of the naming convention, many characters are not compatible with many names such as "spaces" between characters and some special symbols such as " \ " or " * "):

- **Hostname** = Using Alpha-Numeric characters (A-Z and 0-9). Examples would be "PC_17", "Dad_Computer", "Room_012" etc. This type of name is totally arbitrary and can be changed. A simple view of a hostname can be displayed on Windows systems by typing in "hostname" and pressing "enter" when using a CLI.

- **IP Address (Decimal)** = Characters are numeric (0-9) and are arranged in four sections separated by decimals (.) called "Octets". In addition, the primary numbers used in IPv4 networks are between 0 and 255 in each section. Examples are "192.168.1.10" or "169.254.101.20". IP address arrangements appear in many network-related settings on computers, cell phones, televisions, etc. This type of identity can randomly change depending on how the network interface is configured. A simple view of an IP address can be displayed on Windows systems by typing in "ipconfig" and pressing "enter" when using a CLI.

- **Binary** = Binary characters are the foundation of computer and software technology. These characters are represented with either a "0" or a "1". Combinations of binary characters cause actions in software, hardware and identify devices. Often with programming, the two options for bits have specific meanings as in the following:
  - **0 = off, no or false.**
  - **1 = on, yes or true.**
  - Total numbers of combined characters have meaning in elements of instruction, storage and/or speed. Specific well-known combinations have the following names:
    - **Bit** = Single character as in "0" or "1".
    - **Nibble** = Four bits as in "0000" or "1111" or "0101".
    - **Byte (Sometimes called an "Octet")** = Eight bits, or two nibbles as in "11110000"

- **MAC Address (Hexadecimal)** = Also called a "Physical Address" and uses a limited arrangement of Alpha-Numeric characters including only 0-9 and A-F (There are other hexadecimal character combinations but the ones listed are used in network technology). Usually arranged in three groups of four characters separated by decimals or six groups of two characters separated by hyphens (-). Examples would be A9-6F-CE-AA-87-99. The mac-address is actually encoded in the network interface of a device. It is globally unique and more like a network device's "fingerprint". This identity is configured to be permanent and can only be changed by persons with higher levels of electronics, programming or cyber-security experience. A view of a devices physical address can be displayed on Windows systems by typing in "ipconfig /all" and pressing "enter" when using a CLI.

How is a "MAC Address" used?

When working in the field of computer technology it is required to understand at least three identities which computers can use to identify themselves and to be contacted. Those identities are as follows:

- **Hostname** = Appears as a simple word such as "PC1" or "MyComputer".
- **IP address** = Decimal Identity such as "172.16.20.1"
- **Mac Address** = Combination of letters and decimal numbers such as "A8-45-CD-23-FA-BE"

In our present discussion, we will evaluate "MAC Addresses" (**Often stands for "Media Access Control"**). This identity is one the most essential of computer identities. Many people compare the Mac Address to a human "fingerprint". This collection of letter and numbers are globally unique. Essentially, this means that there should be no duplicated Mac address on any network device in the world when the device is produced by a manufacturer. A Mac address is programmed into a ROM chip that is part of the computers "network interface card (NIC)". If the NIC is ever moved to another computer, the MAC will follow the NIC and now be part of the computer of which it is inserted.

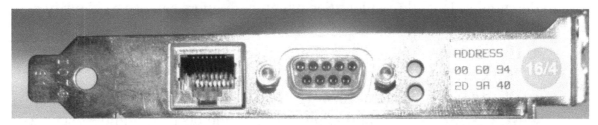

Because the code for the MAC is part of a piece of hardware, we often refer to it as a "Physical Address". In order to view a computers MAC you would utilize the command "IPCONFIG /ALL" such as in the following example:

```
C:\WINDOWS\system32\cmd.exe                                              _ □
      Description . . . . . . . . .   : 3Com EtherLink XL 10/100 PCI For Com
plete PC Management NIC (3C905C-TX) #4
      Physical Address. . . . . . . . : 00-50-DA-5F-77-0C

Ethernet adapter Wireless Network Connection 6:

      Connection-specific DNS Suffix . :
      Description . . . . . . . . . . :
      Physical Address. . . . . . . . : EC-1A-59-B0-B6-DD
      Dhcp Enabled. . . . . . . . . . : Yes
      Autoconfiguration Enabled . . . : Yes
      IP Address. . . . . . . . . . . : 192.168.1.152
      Subnet Mask . . . . . . . . . . : 255.255.255.0
      Default Gateway . . . . . . . . : 192.168.1.1
      DHCP Server . . . . . . . . . . : 192.168.1.1
      DNS Servers . . . . . . . . . . : 192.168.1.1
      Lease Obtained. . . . . . . . . :
      Lease Expires . . . . . . . . . :

C:\>
```

When computers communicate, although IP addresses are configured, most communications occur using the MAC address of the computer. This is because the MAC address is more dependable. The other two identities on computers (i.e., "Hostname" and "IP address") can be easily changed. MAC addresses do not change (Except when a computer uses a "flash update" for repairs or participates in "Spoofing" to attempt to compromise a network). MAC addresses are a total of 12 characters normally separated into groups of two such as the following:

- **CC:CC:CC:MM:MM:MM**
- **CC-CC-CC-MM-MM-MM**

When initial communications occur between servers and other computers, particularly inside a specific LAN, the IP addresses between nodes are used. After a successful communication of some sort occurs, the devices exchange MAC addresses. This allows faster and more stable communications due to a table being used called "ARP (Address Resolution Protocol)". The ARP table is created as successful communications are established between computers.

Chapter 14
IP Addressing Versions and Concepts

IP Addressing Versions and Concepts:

Regardless of the type of software used or the type of computer devices they all require identity information. We discussed the following identities in the section "Nodes, Clients and Identities". Different protocols use many different identities for communication but for our discussions we will primarily discuss "IP Addresses". The following areas will be the focus of the discussion of this book concerning IP addresses:

- **IP Version 4** = One of the primary standards established by ARPANET for network identities on the internet. Although worldwide organizations formally established it in the mid-1980's, IPv4 routes much Internet traffic today and will more than likely exist for quite some time. Elements which allow IPv4's continued existence is in the elements that it is a widely used protocol in data communication and allows compatibility across a number of different network types. Multiple types of computer devices support IPv4 and there are many features such as "Dynamic Host Configuration Protocol", "Vendor Class" and many other utilities. IPv4 is a connectionless protocol which means that the source and destination does not have a dedicated connection but uses intermediary devices to transmit data in a "Relay-Race" fashion. It provides the logical connection between computer devices by providing identification for each device. Due to this configuration, there is a possibility of failed delivery or even duplicated data being sent. Although the protocol has errors inherent in its composition, higher level protocols protect against errors. IPv4 uses a 32-bit (four-byte) method allowing for a total of 2^32 addresses (just over 4 billion addresses). The addresses are converted from binary to decimal when displayed for better understanding for humans. Because of the demand of the growing Internet, the available numbers of remaining addresses were nearing exhaustion anticipated between 2004 and 2011. The problem concerning "lack of available network addresses for the internet" was foreseen many years prior which gave rise to other methods of network addressing for the internet.

- **IP Version 6**= Internet Protocol version 6 (IPv6) is the version of the Internet Protocol (IP) initiated for use near the year 2011 which provides an identification for computers, servers, routers and network devices system across the Internet. IPv6 was developed by the Internet Engineering Task Force (IETF) to address the foreseen exhaustion of available of IPv4 addresses. IPv6 uses a 128-bit address which provides for 2^28 which is a number so large it is said to be an "Undecillion". IPv6 addresses are represented as eight groups of four "Hextets" or "Hexwords" separated by colons such as in the example; "2001:1234:abcd:9944:c6750:cf00:36bb:94ee". The example given in the previous sentence is called "uncompressed" although many times, the full address can be compressed by eliminating groups of zeros.

- **Classfull IP addressing** = Primary method used on the Internet from 1981 to about early 1990's. Using the Classfull method, address spaces are divided into five address classes of "A, B and C" with two more of "D" which is for "multicasting" and "E" reserved for military and experimental purposes. The following chart is an example of Classfull IP addressing:

Traditional Classfull IP Address Standards			
Class	**Leading Octet**	**Subnet Mask**	**Maximum Hosts**
A	0-127	255.0.0.0	16,777,214
B	128 - 191	255.255.0.0	65,534
C	192 - 223	255.255.255.0	254
D	224 - 239	Multicast	NA
E	240 - 247	Military Use	NA

Notes:
1) The "Leading Octet Ranges" display mathematical derivatives including reserved octets.
2) "Maximum Hosts" displays "Usable" hosts and not the pure mathematical derivatives.

- **Classless IP Addressing** = Due to the growth of the internet, there was a need to extend the range of available addressing. IPv6 is a method but the primary restriction to it is that older IPv4 devices could not communicate using IPv6. A solution to the decreasing number of available IPv4 addresses was produced with the implementation of CIDR and VLSM:
  - **Classless Internet Domain Routing (CIDR)** = When networks were developed, traffic was routed based on matching Classfull IP Classes (i.e., "A", "B", "C", etc.) with a specific subnet mask ("255.0.0.0", "255.255.0.0" or "255.255.255.0"). Due to the increase in the number of devices, classfull IP addressing could not support the number of routes on the internet. IPv6 was created, but IPv4 will not understand routing from IPv6. Due to this challenge, programmers began to re-compile router and

switch operating systems to utilize the "binary" form of numbers as opposed to the traditional method of "decimal" utilization. Because of this enhancement, subnet masks can include the following new octets: 128, 192, 224, 240, 248, 252, and 254. These new octets are combined with traditional IP addresses as in the examples below:

CIDR Examples	
Host IP	**Subnet Mask**
204.16.10.54	255.255.255.128
199.240.78.95	255.255.240.0
224.16.76.81	255.255.255.192

- o **Reserved Addresses** = When using IPv4, IPv6 or CIDR, specific types of IP addresses have special uses. We often call these addresses "Reserved" or "Special Use". Regardless of their use, they both have one common element. Reserved IP addresses are not to be used on devices directly connected to the internet (On the Department of Defense backbone). If reserved IP addresses are used on devices which are directly connected to the internet backbone, the situation will result in the device not communicating or a conflict with other devices on the internet. The following are some of the "reserved" addresses:
  - ➤ 169.254.X.Y = Computer systems will self-assign an address within in this range if a DHCP server cannot be contacted.
  - ➤ 192.168.X.Y and 172.16.X.Y = Often used for private networks or training purposes.
  - ➤ 127.0.0.1 = This is called the "loopback" and "localhost" address. This address is used as a utility to ascertain if a computers interface can be contacted by the rest of the network. The loopback is often used if the computers IP address is hidden. Using a "ping" command, a technician

Reserved/Special Use IP Addresses
10.0.0.0 – 10.255.255.255
172.16.0.0 – 172.31.255.255
192.168.0.0 – 192.168.255.255
127.0.0.1 - 127.255.255.254

can perform the following to test if the computer he or she is working on can be contacted by other devices.

➢ Some other reserved IP address appear in the chart below:

Parts of an IP Address:

Based on the communication requirements on a network, various methods of node identification can be used (As in the prior mentioned methods of "hostname", "physical address" and/or "IP address", etc.). When using IP addresses, specific sections of an address have terms which are used to describe their purpose.

- **Network Address/ID** = The section of an IP address which all nodes on a section of a network have in common. Often times, it is the leading numbers on an IP address leading from left to right. An example would be 209.15.X.Y subnet mask of 255.255.0.0. The first two octets identify the network address. Traditionally, the section of the subnet mask will give an idea of the network address because whichever octet section used by the network address ID will reflect the same number of "255's" in the subnet mask.
  - o Think of it like a "last name" on a family. There could be multiple people in a family. Such as the "Smith" family. All of the people in the family could be referred to as "the Smith" family. A computer network or network section uses the network address and it is common on all computers such as in the "Branch Office" network.
- **Host ID/Node ID** = Section of an IP address which is unique for individual systems. This would be like the "first name" of all the people in the "Smith" family. There could be "Bob Smith", "Sam Smith" and "Sally Smith". In reference to a network, think of the following computers:
  - o 172.16.10.10 = Part of the "172.16.10" network but the host ID is "10".
  - o 172.16.10.15 = Part of the "172.16.10" network but the host ID is "15".
  - o 172.16.10.20 = Part of the "172.16.10" network but the host ID is "20".

IP Version 6 Format and Structure:

The display of an IP version 6 address uses what is known as "hexadecimal" characters. These characters include the alpha-numeric values of "A, B, C, D, E, F" and "0, 1, 2, 3, 4, 5, 6, 8 and 9". Remember that any character viewed in a character format is only for the human eye. Computers actually use the "binary" equivalent any displayed character. Below are the listed hexadecimal characters associated with their binary equivalence:

Network Related Numbers Conversion		
Decimal	Hexadecimal	Binary
0	0	0000
1	1	0001
2	2	0010
3	3	0011
4	4	0100
5	5	0101
6	6	0110
7	7	0111
8	8	1000
9	9	1001
10	A	1010
11	B	1011
12	C	1100
13	D	1101
14	E	1110
15	F	1111

Let's look at the various formats and displays of the IPv6 format and characters. IPv6 addresses are written as a string of hexadecimal values. Take the following for example:

2001:1234:EF00:5678:9AAC:DDEE:FF11:ABCD

- Written in full form displays 32 hexadecimal characters.
    - Every 4 bits = Single hexadecimal character.
- Total bits length is 128.
    - Display is separated into eight sections separated by colons.
        - Example as in = $x^1:x^2:x^3:x^4:x^5:x^6:x^7:x^8$.
        - Each "**x**" = 16 bits in or four hexadecimal characters often called "Hextet" or "Hexword"

IPv6 Address Sections:

When using IPv6 it is required to understand the different sections included in the 128-bit identity. Similar to IPv4 sections which include a network section/ID, host section/ID and netmask indicator, IPv6 addresses have sections which provide similar functions but use different names. The following are the sections for IPv6:

- **Prefix** = Often times, internet service providers supply available IPv6 public addresses with the first 64 bits representing the entire network (Often indicated by "/64" appearing after the IP address). This requires every computer on that network to have an identical collection of bits moving from the "Left-to-Right".
  - Utilizes the bits moving from "Left-to-Right" (Often called the "Leftmost Bits").
  - Computers on the same network will have a matching arrangement of "0's" and "1's" on the leftmost side.
  - Expressed with a "/" similar to CIDR.
  - Comparable to an IPv4 subnet mask.
  - Examples of 4 systems in the same network would be as follows:
    - 2001:0db8: fd30:7654:7654:1085:0099:fecc:5871 /64
    - 2001:0db8: fd30:7654:abcd:0052:e433:0001 /64
    - 2001:0db8: fd30:7654:dea0:8766:d222:98cc /64
    - 2001:0db8: fd30:7654:76ff:0433:5432:bb98 /64
      - The "/64" indicates the 1st 64 bits moving from "left-to-right" on all the nodes are identical.

- **Interface ID** = On a flat network, this will be the last 64 bits of the IP address after the Prefix section. This section is used for the unique identifier of the specific node. Below, the section highlighted in "BOLD BLACK" would represent the interface ID. Examples of 4 systems in the same network would be as follows:
  - 2001:0db8:fd30:7654:1085:0099:fecc:5871 /64
  - 2001:0db8:fd30:7654:abcd:0052:e433:0001 /64
  - 2001:0db8:fd30:7654:dea0:8766:d222:98cc /64
  - 2001:0db8:fd30:7654:76ff:0433:5432:bb98 /64

Chapter 15
Example Labs and Configurations

Example Labs and Configurations:

The following are some practical labs illustrating some methods of configuring computers. All listed labs and exercises were created by using actual functioning computers. Some activities may damage or open a computer to various software attacks so it is not recommended to practice on systems that are valuable or needed for everyday purposes. If there are no "disposable" computers available, it is often possible to use software on a functioning computer which allows identical activities of fully manipulating an operating system. These types of programs are often called "Simulators". At the time of this book, there were a number of vendors who supplied simulation software such as "Virtual Box", "Virtual PC", "Hyper-V" and "Packet Tracer". If simulation software is used, some commands used on real devices may not work. Be sure to evaluate simulation software's available functions prior to attempting each lab.

Each lab builds on the prior labs so it is essential that they are completed in the order in which they appear. In addition, each lab increases in challenge levels and repeats prior activities in order to teach procedures and commands thru repetition. As the writer of this text, I would highly recommend completing each lab three times prior to starting the subsequent lab. When performing the lab for the third time, attempt to do so without any notes or instructions.

Hardware Protection during Repairs or Building Computers:

When building computers, it is important to remember that all components must be protected from accidental damage. Some damage is a simple as touching a transistor. In a normal human body, there is stored electricity which could compromise the operation of a computing system. The following are the elements concerning the electricity which may eliminate from a body entitled "ESD":

- **Electrostatic Discharge (ESD):**
  - This is the process of electronic energy to move from a person's body to circuitry on a motherboard. The amount of electricity is identical to the effect of wiping your feet on a carpet and touching someone. The amount of electricity cannot harm a person, but it is just enough to change the electronic settings in a microchip such as RAM, BIOS or even a CPU.

This can in essence "reprogram" parts of a motherboard which could affect data transmission, device communications and event prevent the computer from turning on. There are a number of methods a technician can use to protect from the occurrence of ESD damage to computer such as in the following:

Antistatic Wrist Straps = Essentially, one end of a cable is attached to the wrist of a technician while the other end is clipped to a safe, grounded metal surface such as the case of a computer. This connection allows any static electricity to travel into metal far removed from the circuits on a motherboard.

> **Antistatic Floor Mats** = On the floor of the computer workroom there will be mats which reduce the potential of static electricity accumulation.

> **Self-Grounding** = This is the process of the technician being aware that there may be static electricity accumulated on them and releasing the ESD in a safe manner. Prior to touching any electrical circuit surfaces, after unplugging any live electrical connections, opening the case of the computer, the technician lightly taps the power supply or an unpainted and not circuit board-related surface within the case. Using this method, any potential ESD will be discharged into the protected areas of the computer.

How to Build a Computer:

Contrary to popular belief the process of building a computer is not very difficult. Many people with limited amounts of experience remember long ago when computer technicians had to literally use a material called "solder (A very soft metal used in electronics)" along with a "soldering iron (Used to melt the solder to attach CPU's, transistors and other components to a motherboard)". With present day computer systems this no longer occurs very frequently because systems are designed on what is known as a "Field Replaceable Unit (FRU)" standard. FRU means that a computer technician does not have to solder transistors and small components within a computer but simply replaces an entire part or section with a new part. This allows more rapid repair or construction of computers. The following photo displays the primary parts of a computer system:

- Power Supply
- Optical/DVD drive
- Case, Box or Cabinet
- Drive Bay
- Hard Drive
- SATA Data cables
- Mother Board
- RAM
- CPU with Fan and Heat Sink
- Video Expansion Card

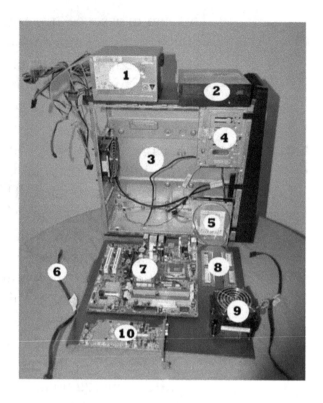

The following pages will provide a brief overview of assembling a computer. At the conclusion you will see how extremely easy the process is. I would strongly encourage any person interested in the field of computer technology and repair to try to build their own system. When learning how to do it however, I strongly suggest that you keep the following cautions in mind:

- **Only use a computer or parts of a computer that are not important!** = There is a chance that you will damage a part that makes the computer unusable. You should not practice on a computer which is used for anyone's everyday activities.
- **Practice on a "cheap" or "inexpensive" computer!** = In many cities and towns there are often "computer shows" where different vendors will lease out a building and set up small versions of their computer stores making available computer parts at a reduced cost. Some of the vendors will be "computer recyclers" who have older computers donated to them. These "used computers" are normally very inexpensive. The recycled computer I will use in the upcoming instructions only cost $30.00. Now keep in mind that an older computer may not work as well as a new system but it will allow

you to get the practice you need to build a computer and install an operating system.

- **Obtain a "Large Form-Factor" computer for practicing!** = A larger computer case will allow you more space to manipulate the components. Form factors which are either "micro" or "mini" often have parts stacked on top of parts or special sections which only allow specific types of components to be inserted. Smaller form factors work well for everyday use but I would recommend a larger one for practice purposes.
- **Have a large "work-table" in a room without carpet!** = This is not to be done on your mother's dining room table! Some of the parts may scratch the surface. In addition, the table should not be on top of carpet. Carpets hold static electricity (Electro-Static Discharge or "ESD") which could damage the motherboard as well as if a small screw drops into the carpet you'll never find it.

Prior to starting a computer's assembly it's a good idea to get together a few tools you will need for construction. There are a number of tool kits which are advertised by different companies ranging from very expensive to absolutely free. There is no "best" toolkit but as a computer technician whatever toolkit you select I recommend it include the following items illustrated in the number picture below:

- **Extra Screws and Standoffs** = You may not have these when you start being a computer technician but they will accumulate as you work. Oftentimes you will buy components which do not include the screws that you will need. At those times this stash of extra screws will be a lifesaver. Standoffs are used to both attach the motherboard to the inside of the case as well as to insulate the motherboard from touching the metal sides of the case.
- **Eyeglass Screwdrivers** = In many computers, specifically laptops there are extremely small screws. Luckily for us they use the same type of screws which appear in eyeglasses. If you attempt to use a normal screwdriver you will damage the screw head and cause yourself a lot of frustration.
- **Tweezer and Small Screw Pincer** = Some components and screws are extremely small and may be difficult to place using your fingers alone. In addition, sometimes small screws will fall into tiny sections of a case or motherboard which are too small for hands to access. These tools can reach in and grab the small screws.

Graphic items 13b and 13c display a pincer as well as when it is "open" ready to grab a screw.

- **Pill Box** = This is often used when disassembling a computer. This allows you to keep track of the actual screws that came out of a computer. It saves you the time of searching through all of your screws for just the right type for whatever component you're installing.
- **Phillips and Flathead Screwdrivers** = Although most screws in computers are phillips head you will occasionally find a flathead screw. In addition, a flathead screwdriver is very useful when manipulating small components which may have to be gently "pried" in some manner as well as removing caps and plugs from what are known as "Jumpers (To be discussed later)".

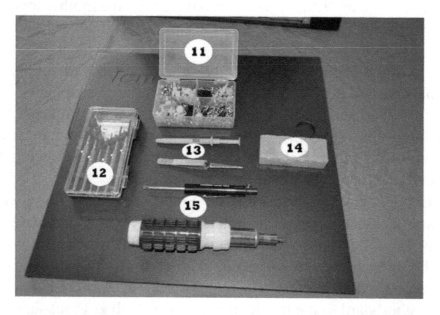

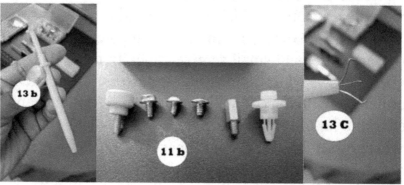

After you have located a table, accumulated the appropriate tools and acquired computer parts you're ready to perform the following operation. The order that appears in this book is not universal and as you get more experience you will perform the tasks in an order that works best for you.

Computer Assembly Steps:

1. **Inspect and open up the case** = You should check the front, back and sides for screws and access ports for optical drives, power supply, audio and USB ports.

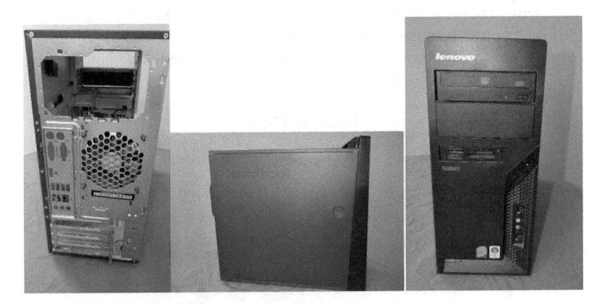

2. **Locate any screws which will allow you to open the case** = Some of the screws may require no tools such as the white "thumbscrew" in the picture below.

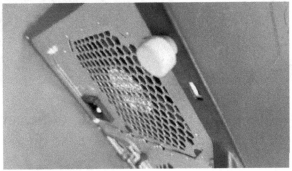

3. **Notice any Drive Bay covers which can be removed** = This case already had a DVD drive in the bay but I have removed it for the example.

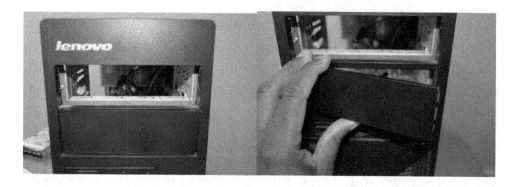

4. **Inspect the inside of the case** = Here you'll find various connectors, wires and drive bays. Make sure that the case you're using has plugs and ports which match the motherboard. In addition, make sure the "holes" on the inside of the case match the arrangement of holes on the motherboard.

Inside of Case

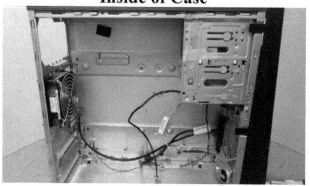

Motherboard Rear Ports   **Case Opening for Ports**

5. **Install Standoffs inside of the case** = If you selected the same form factor for both the motherboard and the case the holes should line up perfectly.

Motherboard Holes   **Standoff Holes**

6. **Install Motherboard** = Take your time and use small angles to insert the board. Gently place the motherboard on top of the standoffs inside the case.

7. **Attach the Motherboard to the case with the screws into the standoffs.**

8. **Locate the Jumper Connections and Cables** = These will provide connections between the outside of the case and the motherboard such as the power button, USB and audio ports. Connect them as necessary.

External Ports

External Port Connector

9. **Connect External Port cable to Motherboard Jumpers**

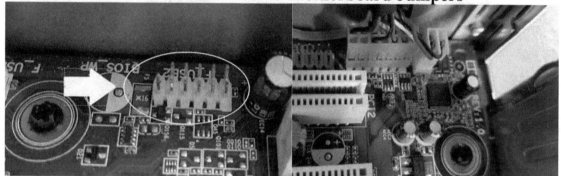

10. **Insert the RAM** = Check the slots for a small "pin" which inserts into a "notch" on the RAM. This ensures that the RAM is not installed backwards. After inserting the RAM there are small "Locking Arms" which will hold the RAM securely.

11.Angle the RAM and press it gently into the slots and lock the arms.

12.Install the CPU, HeatSink and Fan = These components often come connected to one another. When installing the CPU locate the port on the motherboard and assure the pens on the bottom of the CPU lineup appropriately with the holes in the CPU port on the motherboard. There is also a solution called "Thermal Paste" which is put between the CPU and the heatsink. It helps the heat transfer from the CPU to the heatsink.

CPU Port   **Bottom of CPU**

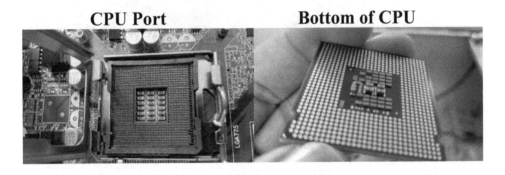

13.Release CPU arm, insert CPU and lock it into place (Observe the "Thermal Paste" on the top of the CPU).

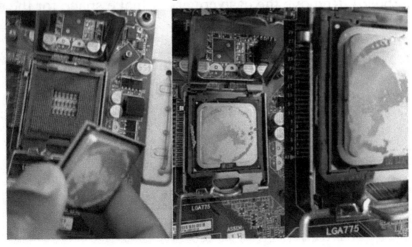

14. **Place the heatsink and fan on top of the CPU and fasten with appropriate screws.**

15. **Plug in HeatSink Fan** = This will provide additional cooling for the CPU.

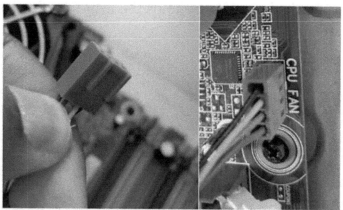

16. **Install any Expansion Cards (i.e., Video Card)** = Locate the expansion panel on the case and the expansion slots available on the motherboard. Remove the case covers to make space for the expansion card you will use.

Expansion Covers Removed (Outside View).

Expansion Cover Removed (Inside View).

17. **Locate the Expansion Slots on the motherboard** = These can be for a number of different cards from PCI to AGP.

Motherboard Expansion Slots
Black Long = Video/Graphic Slot.
White Short = PCI slots (Additional USB, audio and other components).

18. **Install the Video Expansion Card into the AGP slot** = Gently use angles to position the card into the slot as well as the exposed expansion slot panel case opening.

19.Install the Power Supply = Insure that the screw holes on the back of the power supply and the case match. Hold the power supply in position and insert the screws from the back of the case.

Power Supply Screw Holes

Hold Supply Into Place

Fasten Power Supply to Case with Screws

20.Connect Power Supply to the Motherboard = Depending on the motherboard there may be one or multiple electrical connections required. On this motherboard there is a plug for primary power and the CPU.

Main Power	Power Connector	Plugged in

CPU Power Port	CPU Power Plug	CPU Connected

21. Insert Optical/DVD Drive = Most cases have a space identified for optical drives covered with a removable plate and a section which allows the drive to be slid in and secured with screws or a simple clamp.

Front of Case with Panel Removed

Position and slide in the optical drive until it locks or insert screws.

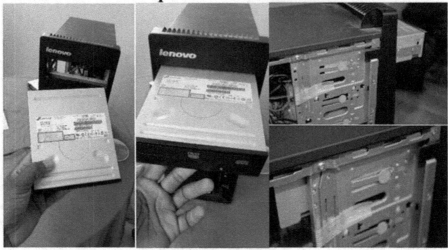

22. **Install the Hard Drive** = In most cases there will also be drive bays for one or more hard drives. These can either have a slide lock mechanism or utilize screws. This unit has a removable hard drive bay. We will have to install the hard drive into the "Drive Caddie" and then install the caddie into the case.

Area to insert the "Hard Drive Caddie".

Insert hard drive into Caddie.

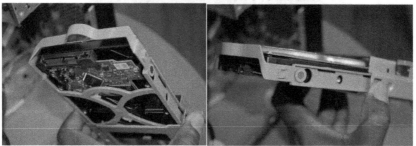

Angle and lock hard drive caddie into position.

23. **Connect Data and Power Cables to Drives** = The power supply will have preexisting power cables and the optical and hard drives should come with data cables. With the type of components were using the cables will be of the "SATA" type. The cables are plugged in almost side-by-side on most devices.

Sata Power Connector   **Data Connector**

Connect the power and data cables into the hard drive.

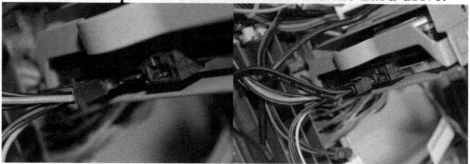

Repeat the same activities with the Optical/DVD drive.

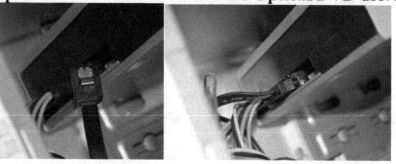

24. **Connect Sata Data cables to motherboard** = On recent motherboards there are two or more Sata ports available for connections.

25.The results of the assembly looks like the next photo. Complete the assembly process by closing up the tower.

To make the system ready there are a few remaining tasks such as connecting a monitor, keyboard and mouse. After that all the physical work is done. Remember however, if the computer is turned on it will not display exact information if a particular part is assembled incorrectly or if they are not compatible. Depending on the problem you can either get audio or visual indicators, however. The following are not comprehensive but possible examples of errors warnings you may encounter when building a computer:

- **Quick "Beeps" and a pause repeatedly** = RAM is not detected. This could be caused by unlocked or incompatible RAM.
- **Long "Beep" followed by two short repeatedly** = Video card is not found.
Black screen with blinking line in upper left-hand corner = No operating system exists to load. Don't be afraid, this is could be a good thing if you are building a computer for the first time. It means all your parts are assembled correctly but the computer cannot do anything. The screen might look like the following photo:

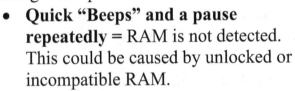

After the assembly of the computer it is necessary to install an operating system. There are multiple ways to install an operating system with the two most frequent is using either an optical disk such as a DVD or using an ISO on a USB device such as a flash drive. Performing a USB installation requires some advance technical ability such as making the USB drive bootable as well as configuring the computer itself to boot-up off of the USB Port. For most beginning technicians the DVD method is primarily used.

USB or DVD OS Install Options

Installing an Operating System

When building a computer after all the physical hardware has been assembled an operating system must be installed. Below are a few options for installation as well as challenges a technician may encounter in the process:

- **DVD** = This is the most traditional and well-known method for installing an operating system. A challenge in this method is when the computer does not have an optical drive. In addition, many operating systems require "Dual-Sided" DVDs for installation because of the large amount of data the operating system includes. Some optical drives do not recognize dual-sided media. Also, the speed of the installation is affected by the rotation speed of the optical drive. Lastly, if there are scratches on the DVD the installation could fail.

- **Network or PXE (Pre-Boot Execution)** = This method is often used when there are a large number of computers to be installed simultaneously. This method requires an established network infrastructure of cabling, servers, switches and other items. This also requires a lot of expertise of the technician.

- **Boot USB Drive** = High-experience technicians prefer this method because there are many ways to customize installations and utilities. Challenges include creating a USB drive that can turn on and interact with a computer without the computer having an existing operating system. In addition, the computer must have the ability to boot-up from an attached USB device.

The process for installing an operating system has about 8 steps performed in sequence. It is not a very difficult operation and is very similar between various versions of operating systems. The following will display an installation of Windows 7 but the process is similar when installing higher versions such as Windows 8 thru Server 2016. To begin the process of installing the operating system you must have the files on a bootable USB drive or optical media such as a DVD. If using a USB flashdrive, you will plug the flash drive into any available USB port, turn on the computer and activate the "Boot Sequence" from the BIOS by tapping the appropriate key on the keyboard (Sometimes the key will be "F10", "F12" or "Del"). If using a DVD or optical media you will have to momentarily power-on the computer, open the DVD tray and insert the DVD. After which you must "re-power" or "reset" to reboot the computer. When using a DVD as the computers BIOS realizes it has no operating system on the hard drive it will immediately search for the DVD drive to provide one. After the installation files are located on the DVD the following installation will occur:

1. **Installation files load into RAM** = The initialization files will begin to be expanded into memory displaying a "loading" notification followed by a "Starting Windows" logo and a "Install Now" dialogue box.

2. **Country and Keyboard Customization** = The installation requests this information in order to configure the language to display on the screen as and the position of the keys on the keyboard.

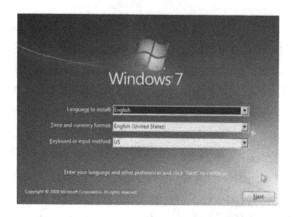

3. **End-License User Agreement** = This is a mandatory dialogue which must have a "Accept" checkmark placed in the box or installation will not continue.

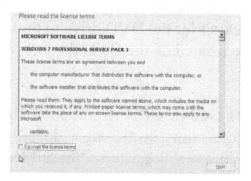

4. **Installation Type Options** = If you select "Upgrade" the installation will attempt to preserve all previous programs in the event you were installing the operating system on an already functioning computer (There are always functions that no longer operate when you do this). By selecting the "Custom" option if there were any preexisting files or programs on the computer they will all be eliminated. This is the option used when building a brand-new computer often referred to as a "Clean Install".

5. **Installation Location** = It is possible to have multiple volumes on one hard drive or a computer with multiple hard drives. This interface allows you to select exactly which volume or hard drive you would like to use. Notice that it also displays the size of the drive.

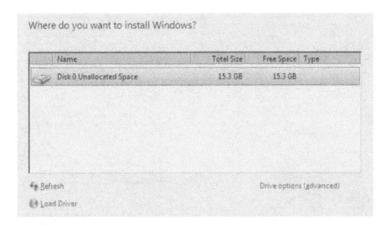

6. **Installation files expand and are deposited on the hard drive** = At this stage the files in RAM begin to copy necessary operating system files from the DVD onto the hard drive. Depending on the speed of your computer this process can take between 10 and 30 minutes. After the necessary files have been copied the hard drive the computer will reboot two or three times (**Note**: If you see the message "Press any key to boot from DVD" do not do so. If you do, the installation process will start all over).

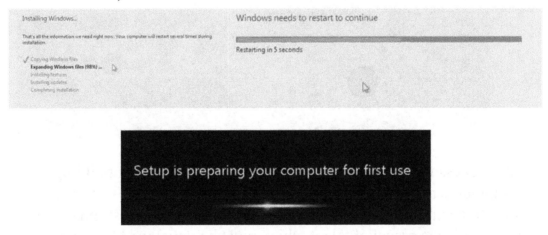

7. **User Customization and Time Zones** = After all the installation files have been loaded into the hard drive the system reboots and asks more questions about the name of the computer, the primary person who will control the computer and offer to create a password for that person. In

addition, it will ask what level of firewall protection should be used, the time zone the computer exists in and if the installing person would like the operating system to check for any updates available for the operating system from Microsoft.

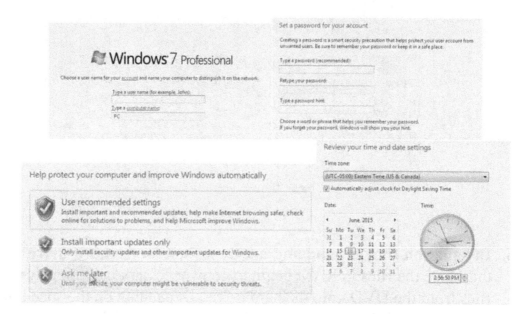

8. **Finishing Installation** = After all the settings and files are configured from the previous questions the installation begins the "First Run" tasks to design the desktop and Start Menu for the present user after which it is displayed and the computer is fully functional.

The process for installing an operating system as well as building a computer is not very complex as illustrated previously. The ability to select the appropriate components and then to further customize the software is the essential talent which must be developed by a person working on computers. The skill to configure and manage computer technology is not just a science but it is more like an "art form".

Make USB Flashdrive Bootable with DiskPart:

Listed below is a method a technician can use to create a USB drive which can boot a computer as well as install an operating system. In the following exercise it is recommended that you have a USB drive greater than 5 Gigabytes in order to fully store an ISO or the files for an operating system copied from a DVD (It is possible to use a smaller drive if you're practicing with smaller OS's or repair utilities based upon Linux or other platforms). Understand that all previous files on the USB drive will be completely deleted. After you have completed the process however you can continue storing files on the flashdrive and it will retain its ability to boot-up a computer. The following are items you will need:

- o Functioning computer with a Windows Operating System (Windows 8 thru 10 or even Server 2008 thru 2016).
- o Administrative rights on that Windows computer.
- o DVD or ISO of a Windows operating system (Windows 8 thru 10 or even Server 2008 thru 2016).
- o Large capacity USB flashdrive or an external USB hard drive.

PLEASE NOTE, the following instructions can cause extreme damage to a computer or USB drive. It is recommended that the steps be performed on a computer and USB drive which has no valuable data on it and is primarily used for practice.

1. Start the process by activating a command line as an "Administrator" on a working Windows computer (Go to "Windows System" and "right-click" on "Command Prompt" and then "left-click on "More" and "Run As Administrator").

2. The prompt will display "c:\windows\system32" as illustrated below:
3. Activate the disk partitioning utility in Windows by typing "diskpart" and notice the utility engages:

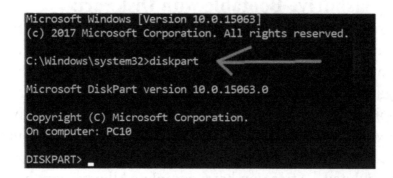

4. To continue, type in "list disk" (Note: there <u>is a space between</u> the two words) which will display all the drives your system presently has access to:

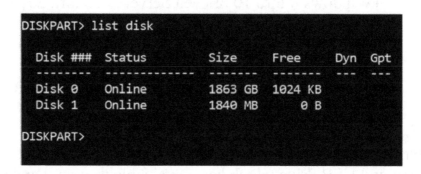

5. The drives are listed as "Disk 0", "Disk 1" and so on. Traditionally, "Disk 0" is your "C:\" drive or the volume which hosts the operating system and other disks are ones you have connected. Pay special attention to the sizes of the disks listed. Normally, the smallest will be the USB drive (In my case it is "Disk 1"). To continue type in "select disk 1 (Use the disk number of the one displayed on your computer. It may not be the same as my example)". After directing the diskpart utility to the appropriate disk (Drive) perform the following commands:
   - ☐ clean (Permanently erases the USB drive (Make sure it is the correct one!!!)
   - ☐ create partition primary (Creates a partition table on the USB drive.)
   - ☐ select partition 1 (Focus the utility on the new partition.)
   - ☐ active (Configure the USB drive as primary and able to operate with a BIOS or UEFI.)

    ☐ format fs=fat32 (Establishes the file system on the USB drive. Depending on the size of the drive this may take some time.)

    ☐ exit = Turns off diskpart.

6. Now it is possible to either copy the contents from a Windows operating system DVD or an entire ISO to the USB drive. To utilize the new Bootable USB drive perform the following:

    ☐ Assure a computer is turned off.

    ☐ Insert the USB drive into any available port.

    ☐ Turn on the computer while tapping whichever key allows the "Boot Menu" to appear (Such as "F10", "F12" or the "Del" key).

    ☐ An option related to "Boot from USB Device" will display on the computers screen. Press the associated key and the system will start from the USB drive and initiate the installation of the operating system.

Renaming Computer Creating, Activating and Deleting Users:

The following will display a process used daily by computer technicians. We will illustrate a process to identify a computer, install user accounts and even removing particular accounts. The following list is not all-inclusive and the associated videos are more detailed.

1) **Identify the computers name using two methods:**
    o CLI command "hostname".
    o Right-Click on "This PC" and select "Properties".

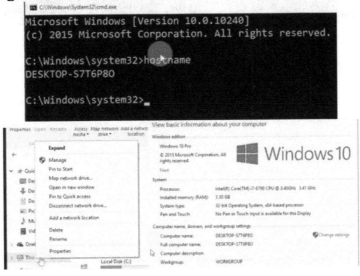

2) Start Process of Renaming Computer.

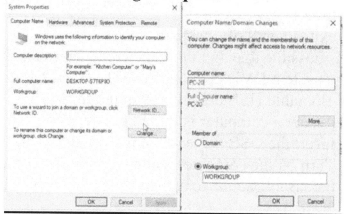

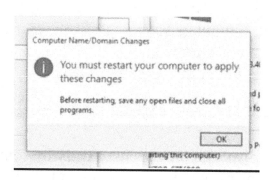

3) After computer restarts, check for name either way.

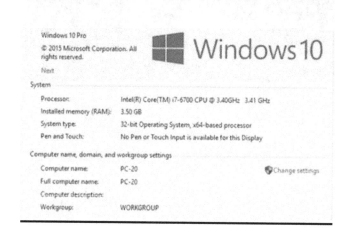

Creating Users on a Windows 10 Computer (Non-Domain Client):

The following will display a process used daily by computer technicians. We will illustrate a process to install user accounts on a computer running Windows 10 without any associated with a controlling Server. The following list is not all-inclusive and the associated videos are more detailed.

1) **Right-Click on "This PC" to start and then select "Manage".**

2) **This will activate "Computer Management". Navigate to "Local Users and Groups".**
3) **Go to "Users" and view users that already exist.**

4) **Create "CCP1" with a password of "Password1".**

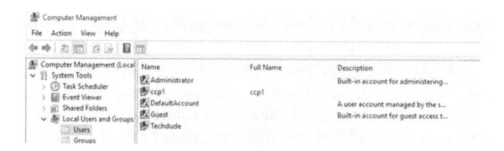

5) Sign Out and login as the new user (CCP1).

Configuring Disk Quotas on a Windows Computer:

Although multiple users can exist on a specific computer there is the potential that one user will use up most of the available space on a hard drive. To prohibit the use of any person taking up all available hard drive space there is the option of enabling "Disk Quotas". Essentially this limits the amount of space available on a high drive for particular user or all users on a computer. This function is available in operating systems as far back as Windows XP. To access Disk Quotas the following would be the appropriate steps:

1) Locate the "C:\" drive on the computer.

2) Bring up the "Properties Menu" by "right-clicking" on the "C:\"
    drive and then go to the "Properties" option.

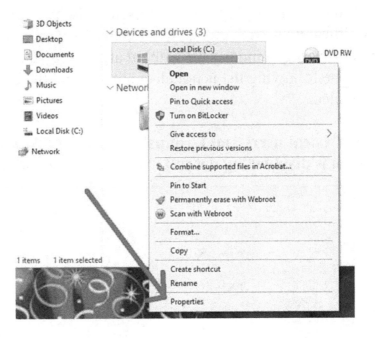

3) A property sheet will appear with a number of tabs at the top.
    Select the "Quota" tab to display quota settings for the "C\:" drive.
    Notice that there are a number of options available such as
    prohibiting users from exceeding a specific amount of data or
    simply issuing a warning to a user who has exceeded a specified
    storage amount. After quotas have been enabled it is possible to
    use the "Quota Entries" button to display exactly how much space
    individual users are presently taking up.

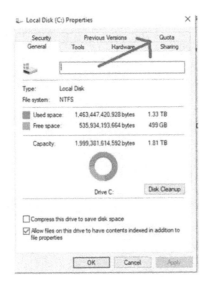

Activating an Account on Windows 10 Computer (Non-Domain Client):

The following will display a process used daily by computer technicians. We will illustrate a process to activate a disabled user account on a computer running Windows 10 without any associated with a controlling Server. The following list is not all-inclusive and the associated videos are more detailed.

1) Go to "Local users and Groups" and select "Administrator" (Which is disabled by default. Notice the "down" facing arrow):

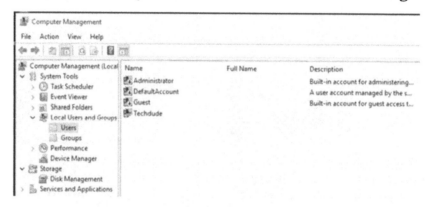

2) Make his password our normal "Password1".

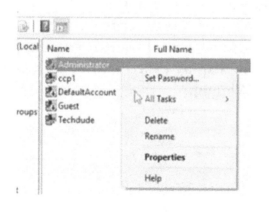

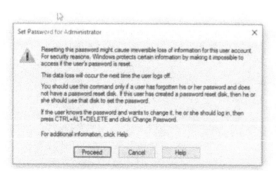

3) Sign off and Login as "Administrator"

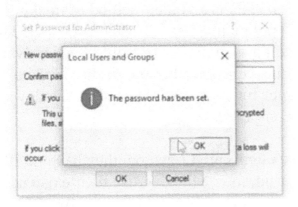 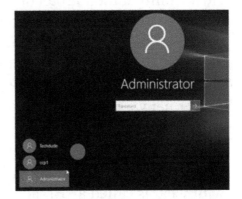

Deleting an Account on Windows 10 Computer (Non-Domain Client):

The following will display a process used daily by computer technicians. We will illustrate a process to delete a user account on a computer running Windows 10 without any associated with a controlling Server. The following list is not all-inclusive and the associated videos are more detailed.

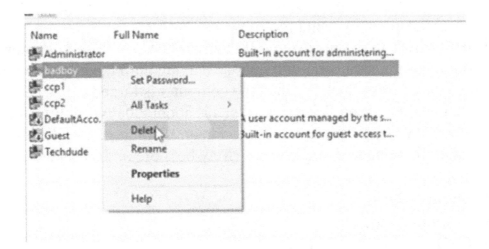

Confirm DHCP address on Windows Computer:

Often times, there are hundreds of computers which require addresses on a network. Not only is it an immense task to manually configure each computer, but there is a great possibility that duplicate addresses will be applied to multiple computers which can hamper and even disable entire networks. Due to this requirement of networks, there are methods in which computers can receive an address from a computer normally called a "DHCP" or "BOOTP" server. DHCP is an abbreviation for "Dynamic Host Configuration Protocol". "BOOTP" is an older method of tracking and distributing addresses and will not be illustrated in this text. A DHCP device or "Server" can be an operating system on a computer or simply a device which performs the addressing function. For our discussion, we will concentrate on the DHCP Server function implemented in Windows Server networks as they relate to computers.

On most computer networks, when clients are turned on, they have no IP address settings. During their boot-up, they will advertise their existence with what is called a "Broadcast" which is a "Scream to the Network" that the computer would like an IP address given to it. The broadcast is associated with the "physical" or "MAC" address of the device (i.e., "3D-44-AC-FC-55-66"). Often the "broadcast" address appears in the following forms (In IPv4 and Hexadecimal):
- "0.0.0.0"
- "255.255.255.255"
- "FF-FF-FF-FF-FF-FF"

The signal is "heard" by a "DHCP" server which in turn, sends an IP address to the client by using the "physical" address as the target. Once the client agrees to use the offered IP address, the DHCP server records the address as given out and will not use it again until the client no longer requires the address, such as when the computer is turned off. The default time that is often set on Windows clients is about 8 days, but this time can be shortened or lengthened. In addition to an IP address, the client is also given the following network settings (May be more or less depending on the network):
- **Subnet Mask**
- **Domain Name**
- **Default Gateway location.**
- **Domain Name Server location.**

Oftentimes, a device will fail at receiving an IP address for a multitude of reasons. Using CLI commands, it is possible to ascertain if a computer was unsuccessful in IP attainment. Using the normal utility "ipconfig", if the address appears with the first two octets of "169.254.x.y" and a subnet mask of "255.255.0.0" the following is assumed:
- **The computer is connected to a network.**

- **Electronically, the network card interface and all associated cables are connected.**
- **The client was not able to receive and address from a DHCP server.**

The ip address of "169.254.x.y" is defined as "APIPA" (Automatic Private IP Addressing). This is the result of the process of a computer giving itself an IP address due to inability to communicate with a DHCP server. Prior to assigning itself an IP address, the client will use "ICMP" (Internet Control Messaging Protocol) to "Ping" an IP address it desires to use in the "169.254.x.y" range. If no other device responds, the client will use the address. "Ping" is a CLI network utility often used in computer troubleshooting. The command will display if a specific computer has the ability to be contacted. The format to use the command is as follows:

- **Ping <ip address of target computer>**

Below is a display of a ping when a device is successfully contacted. Depending on the operating systems, successful detection of a computer will render 3 to 8 "positive" replies:

If a device is not located, the following would be the response:

Many times, computer technicians require more than 3 to 8 responses regardless of if they are positive or negative. In this situation, a "switch" to the "ping" option is utilized which will cause the ping to continue until manually terminated (Often called an "extended" or "infinite" ping). To terminate an extended ping, the control key combination "Ctrl+C" must be performed. The format and an illustration are as follows:

```
C:\WINDOWS\system32\cmd.exe

C:\>ping 98.139.180.149 -t

Pinging 98.139.180.149 with 32 bytes of data:

Reply from 98.139.180.149: bytes=32 time=34ms TTL=50
Reply from 98.139.180.149: bytes=32 time=46ms TTL=50
Reply from 98.139.180.149: bytes=32 time=34ms TTL=50
Reply from 98.139.180.149: bytes=32 time=51ms TTL=50
Reply from 98.139.180.149: bytes=32 time=46ms TTL=50
Reply from 98.139.180.149: bytes=32 time=26ms TTL=50
Reply from 98.139.180.149: bytes=32 time=21ms TTL=50
Reply from 98.139.180.149: bytes=32 time=26ms TTL=50
Reply from 98.139.180.149: bytes=32 time=33ms TTL=50
Reply from 98.139.180.149: bytes=32 time=24ms TTL=50

Ping statistics for 98.139.180.149:
    Packets: Sent = 10, Received = 10, Lost = 0 (0% loss),
Approximate round trip times in milli-seconds:
    Minimum = 21ms, Maximum = 51ms, Average = 34ms
Control-C
^C
C:\>_
```

Configuring an IP address on a Server or Client:

The following is an example using a Windows GUI to establish a Static IP Address on a network interface. The listed steps are not all-inclusive. More detailed instructions are displayed in the videos associated with this exercise.

1) **Access the computers icon entitled "Network and Sharing Center".**

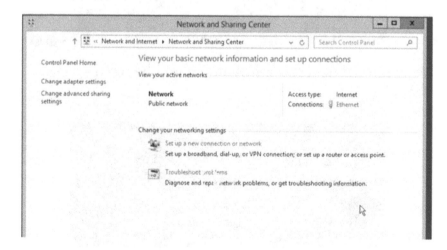

2) **Click on the Icon (Words) which read "Change Adaptor Settings".**

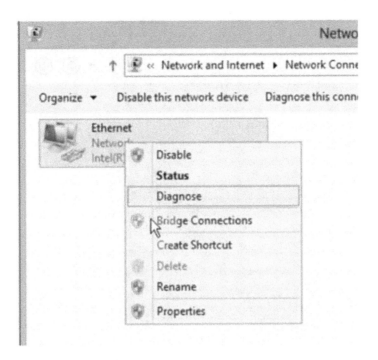

3) Locate the Network Interface (Listed here as "Ethernet") and "Right-Click on it to reveal the properties menu. Afterwards, click on "Properties".

4) Select the WORD (Do not uncheck the box!) for "Internet Protocol Version 4" and click "Properties" in the lower right corner. Continue to fill out the fields with the following settings you require.

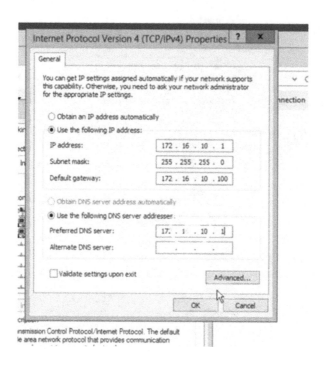

5) **After inserting the desired IP address, click "OK" and close out all the other windows. If you like, you can open a "command prompt" and type "ipconfig" to assure the IP address is established.**

Using a CLI to Manually Configure an IP Address (On Windows Systems):

Depending on the device or operating system, in order to communicate with other computers, there is the requirement for settings which allow transmission and reception of signals. In order for this to occur, devices must share methods of communications commonly referred to as "Protocols". There are multiple protocols used in present computer technology. The discussions in this text will primarily revolve around the protocol classified as TCP/IP (Transmission Control Protocol/Internet Protocol). This method of communication has two presently utilized version of version 4 and version 6. Much of our discussion will relate to version 4. In addition, many of the sections discussed will be directly related to Microsoft Operating Systems as well as the Cisco IOS.

When utilizing computers which have a Windows Operating System, there are both GUI and CLI methods of viewing and manipulating computer configurations. When using CLI, the command prompt is activated and then we will use the command IPCONFIG. When using this command in its smallest format, the CLI displays basic computer settings.

```
C:\WINDOWS\system32\cmd.exe                                    _ □ x

C:\>ipconfig

Windows IP Configuration

Ethernet adapter Local Area Connection 3:

        Media State . . . . . . . . . . . : Media disconnected
Ethernet adapter Local Area Connection 5:

        Media State . . . . . . . . . . . : Media disconnected
Ethernet adapter Wireless Network Connection 6:

        Connection-specific DNS Suffix   . :
        IP Address. . . . . . . . . . . . : 192.168.1.152
        Subnet Mask . . . . . . . . . . . : 255.255.255.0
        Default Gateway . . . . . . . . . : 192.168.1.1

C:\>
```

When performing the basic command of IPCONFIG the following are explanations of the display:

- **IP Address** = Decimal identity of computer on a TCP/IP network.
- **Subnet Mask** = Provides segmentation of groups of computers.
- **Default-Gateway** = Point which allows a section of a network to communicate with devices outside of that network.

The command also has optional modifications available which will show more specific displays of computer configurations or allow the use of advanced features and tasks. In order to use the enhanced features, additional words and characters must be appended to the command. The character which must be added is often called a "Forward Slash" or a "Switch" normally represented by using "/". The "Switch" is followed by a number of other commands which can perform a number of operations. The most common enhanced command is by adding the "All" perimeter. This command will display a complete readout of all the settings presently used by the windows client as follows:

```
C:\WINDOWS\system32\cmd.exe                                          - □ ×

C:\>ipconfig /all

Windows IP Configuration

        Host Name . . . . . . . . . . . . : 3Com
        Primary Dns Suffix  . . . . . . . :
        Node Type . . . . . . . . . . . . : Hybrid
        IP Routing Enabled. . . . . . . . : No
        WINS Proxy Enabled. . . . . . . . : No
        DNS Suffix Search List. . . . . . : router.home

Ethernet adapter Local Area Connection 3:

        Media State . . . . . . . . . . . : Media disconnected
        Description . . . . . . . . . . . : Realtek PCIe GBE Family Controller
        Physical Address. . . . . . . . . : 40-09-4F-06-09-DD

Ethernet adapter Local Area Connection 5:

        Media State . . . . . . . . . . . : Media disconnected
        Description . . . . . . . . . . . : 3Com EtherLink XL 10/100 PCI For Com
plete PC Management NIC (3C905C-TX) #4
        Physical Address. . . . . . . . . : 00-09-4F-5F-DD-09-4F

Ethernet adapter Wireless Network Connection 6:

        Connection-specific DNS Suffix  . : router.home
        Description . . . . . . . . . . . : Belkin USB Adaptor
        Physical Address. . . . . . . . . : EC-09-4F-B0-B6-DD
        Dhcp Enabled. . . . . . . . . . . : Yes
        Autoconfiguration Enabled . . . . : Yes
        IP Address. . . . . . . . . . . . : 192.168.1.152
        Subnet Mask . . . . . . . . . . . : 255.255.255.0
        Default Gateway . . . . . . . . . : 192.168.1.1
        DHCP Server . . . . . . . . . . . : 192.168.1.1
        DNS Servers . . . . . . . . . . . : 192.168.1.1
        Lease Obtained. . . . . . . . . . : Saturday, August 12, 2007 7:40:59 AM

        Lease Expires . . . . . . . . . . : Sunday, August 13, 2007 7:40:59 AM

C:\>_
```

IP addresses are essential in computer communications on TCP/IP networks. There are a number of methods utilized to establish address settings on network. The following are some of the options:

- **Static Address (Manual)** = This allows an IP address to be established by a technician. The technician can either use a CLI or GUI to manually type in an IP address. To set an IP address using CLI, the following could be done:
  - **netsh interface ipv4 set address name="3Com19111" static 100.100.100.10 255.255.255.0 100.100.100.100**

The above command inserted "100.100.100.10" as the computer's IP address with a subnet mask of 255.255.255.0 and a default-gateway setting of 100.100.100.100. To set an IP address using the GUI, the following would be performed:

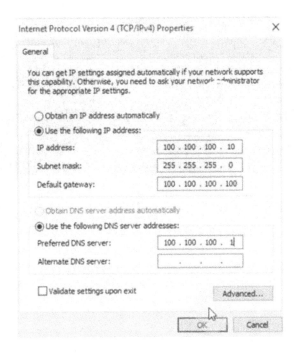

Adding a Printer to a Server or Windows 10 Computer:

*Notes: You must be logged in as "Administrator" to perform the actions required for this task. The following is an example of using a method of adding a printer to a Windows Operating System Computer. The listed steps are not all-inclusive. More detailed instructions are displayed in the videos associated with this exercise.

1) Locate "Control Panels" using either the "Search Option", "Start Menu" or the "Apps" Snap-in.

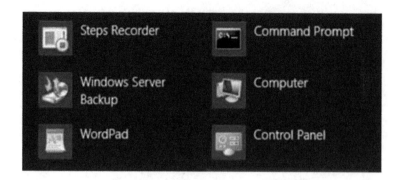

2) Locate "Control Panels" using either the "Search Option", "Start Menu" or the "Apps" Snap-in.

Adjust your computer's settings

System and Security
Review your computer's status
View event logs

Network and Internet
View network status and tasks

Hardware
View devices and printers
Add a device

Programs
Uninstall a program
Turn Windows features on or off

3) Locate "Hardware" which allows the adding of printers. Only the default icons are available. Go to the menu bar and select "Add a Printer".

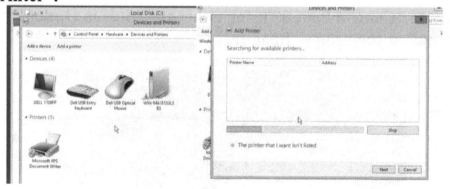

4) A "Printer Searching" wizard will activate. You can click "Stop". Click the Radio button to "Add a Local Printer or Printer with Manual Settings".

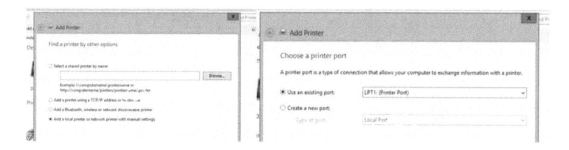

5) Select "Use existing Port" and use "LPT1" (This will work for this exercise). The Windows Operating System comes equipped with many basic drivers for several printers. Use the "Manufacturer" window and select "HP". Then, in the "Printers" window, select any "LaserJet 4000 Series" printer between 4000 and 4999 (Their drivers are the easiest for our exercises).

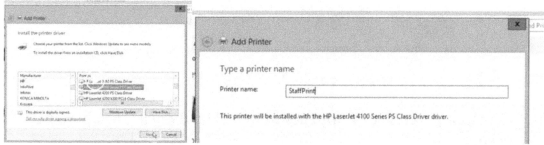

6) We will replace the printers name with the name "StaffPrint". We want to allow other computers to use the printer on the network so it is required to give it a "Share Name". We will use the same name the printer has been given previously.

7) If this was an actual printer, we can send a test page to view our success. For our exercise, it is not needed so just click "Finished".

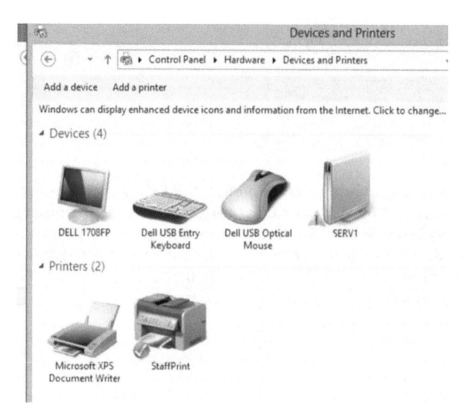

8) Our new printer now appears under "Hardware", ready to be used.

Creating a File Share on Windows 10 Non-Domain Client:

With this example, we will totally disable all security to make access easier. When you work on a computer in an office environment, the settings will be more customized. The following list is not all-inclusive and the associated videos are more detailed.

1) **Make sure all firewalls are off.**

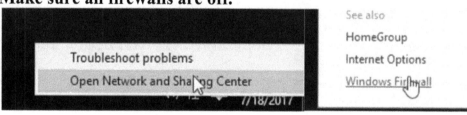

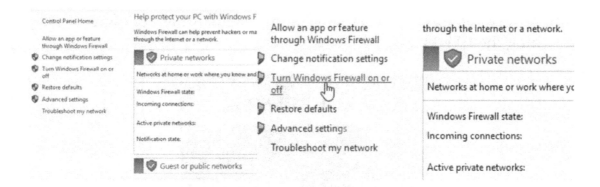

2) Make all the "Green" icons turn "Red".

3) Turn off "Password Protection".

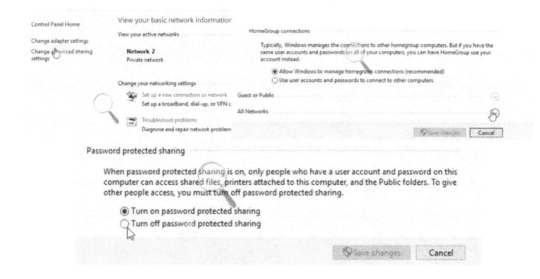

4) **Assure you have the correct IP address and other computers can ping the IP address.**

5) **Create needed folders inside of "C" drive (Some of these folders are used for other exercise).**

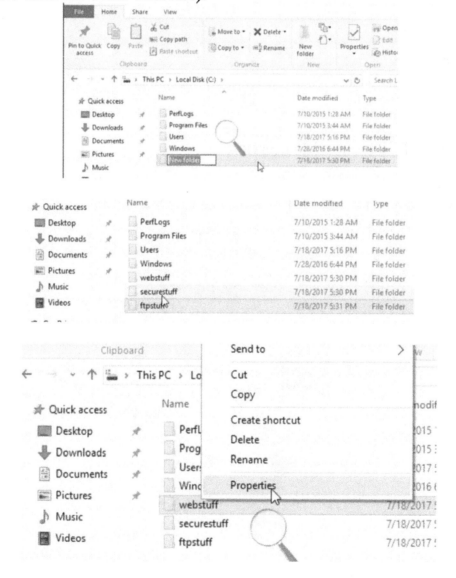

6) Configure "Share" permissions on each folder.

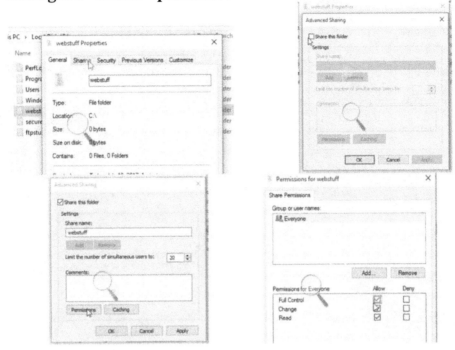

7) Configure "Security" permissions on each folder.

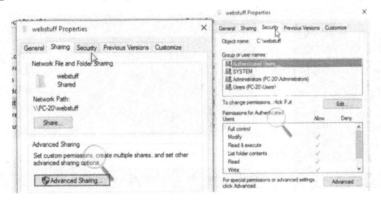

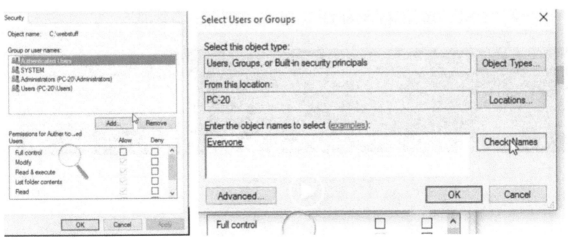

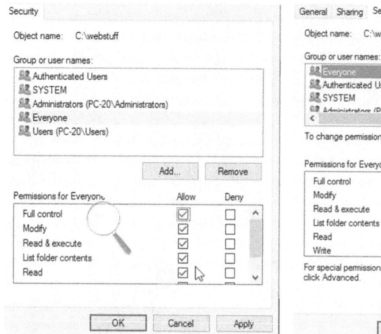

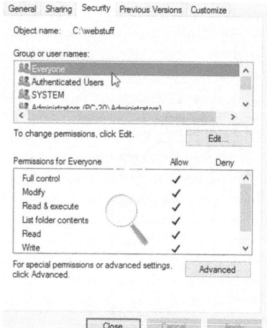

8) Check to assure that the folders are shared two ways:

➢ **"Net Share" utility:**

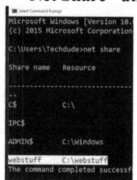

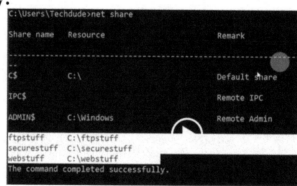

➢ **"UNC" method (Get IP Address first):**

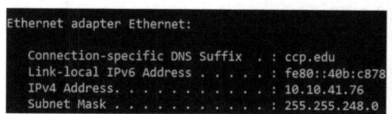

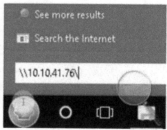

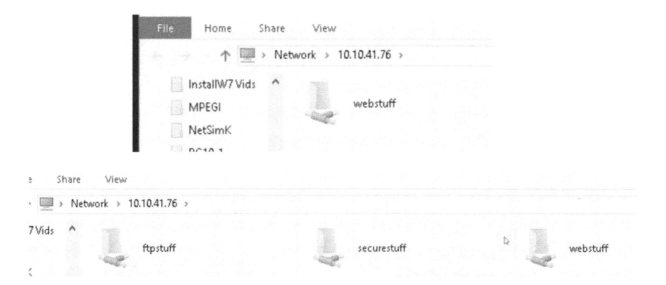

9) **Now anyone on the network who can "ping" your computer will be able to access any files you place in the shared folders.**

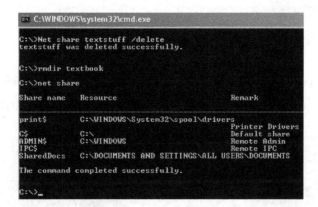

Creating a Shared Resource using the Explorer GUI:

When using a GUI, it is required to create or locate the resource, activate the resources' "property sheet" and configure "sharename", "permissions" and "security" settings. The following is an abbreviated example of using a GUI for simple sharing of a directory. More detailed steps are provided in the examples section of this text.

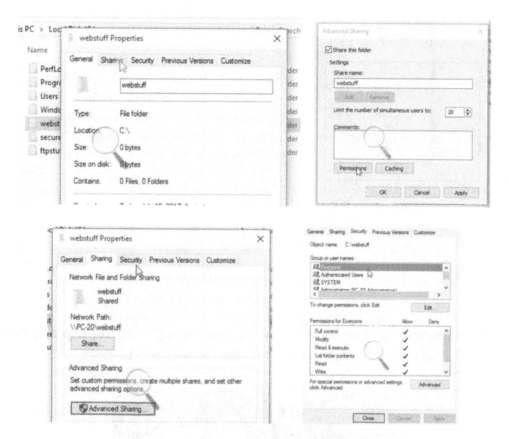

1) **Check the availability of the shared resource by using the "computer identity" portion of the UNC in the "run" option.**

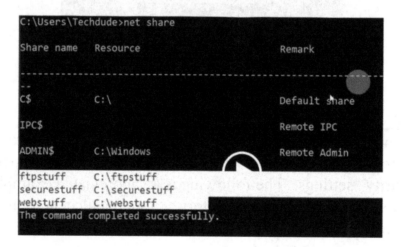

2) **To remove the share, repeat the actions and utilize the "remove" option under "Folder shared"**

Creating a Shared Resource using the CLI:

When using the CLI, the following are commands utilized:

1) **CD** = This is a helping command to move you to the root of whichever drive you are using.
2) **Mkdir <Desired name of directory>** = This creates a directory.
3) **Net share <Desired Name of Share>=<DriveLocation and name of directory to share>** = This makes the directory accessible from the network.
4) **Net share** = This command without following parameters displays any shared directories or resources on your system.

The following is an example of creating a share and assuring its existence using a CLI:

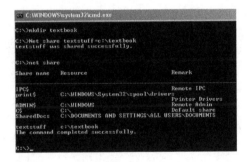

To eliminate the share via command line, perform the following:

1) **Cd** = As stated before, moving to the root of the drive.
2) **net share <sharename> /delete** = This command removes the share function.
3) **Rmdir <directory name>** = This command will delete the directory.

Configuring Encryption for Users (Windows 7 or Windows 10):

*Notes: You must be logged in as "Administrator" to perform the actions required for this task. The following is an example of using a security method combining "Encryption" and a "Public Key Infrastructure". The listed steps are not all-inclusive. More detailed instructions are displayed in the videos associated with this exercise.

1) **You must install encryption software that can create Public and Private Keys such as "Gpg4Win" which will enable a program called "Kleopatra".**

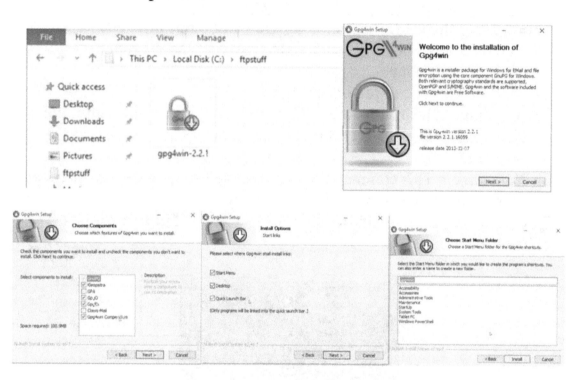

2) **After Installing "GPG4Win" you will notice a new icon called "Kleopatra".**

3) **Use this interface to create a PKI and store it to location other users can access to install it into their version of "Kleopatra".**

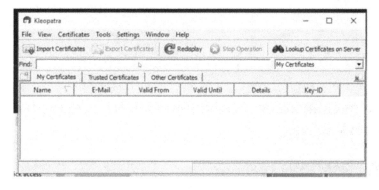

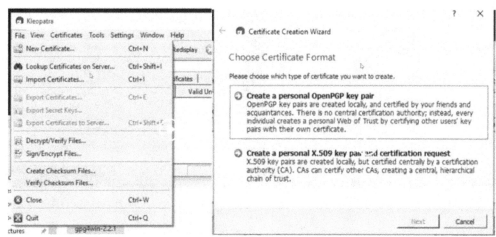

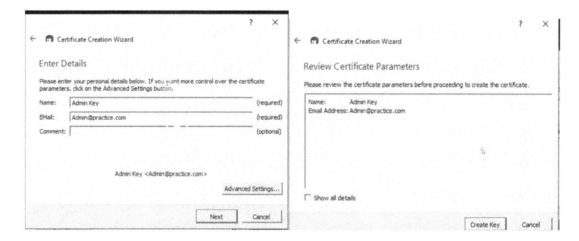

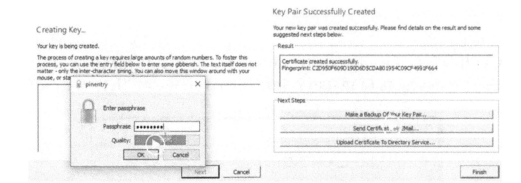

4) Create a document, encrypt it and store the encrypted version in the network drive.

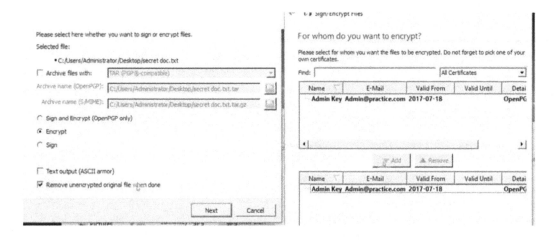

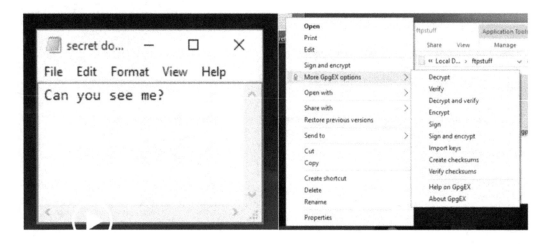

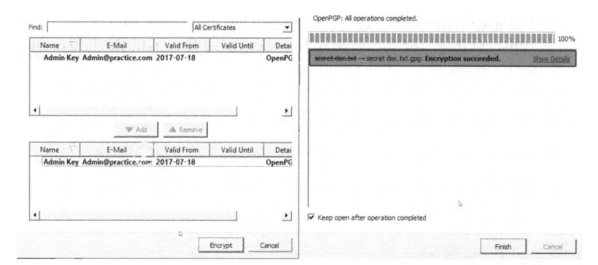

5) Sign-out and login as another user. You notice that the other user has "Kleopatra" but it has no keys. Copy both the "PKI" and the "Encrypted Document" to the desktop.

secret
doc.txt.gpg

6) Try to open the "encrypted document" and it fails. If you select "Notepad" to open it, the characters are illegible.

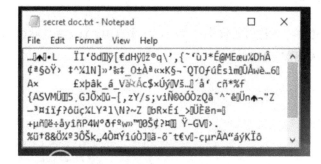

7) **The user requires the correct "public key" in order to "unscramble" the message in the encrypted file. Add the key to the user's account.**

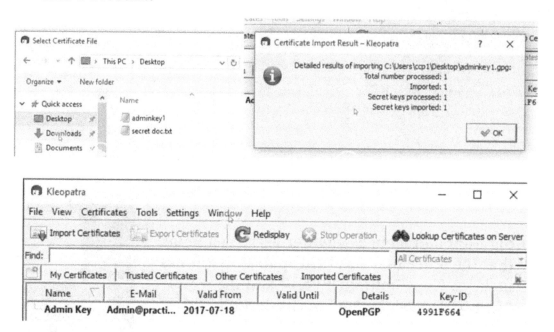

8) **Decrypt the encrypted file using the appropriate key and passphrase.**

9) **The decryption will require you to input the passcode the original owner of the key used.**

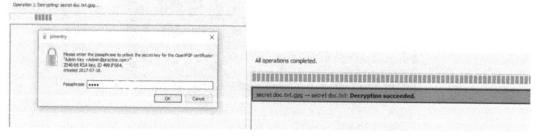

10) Now this user will be able to read the file.

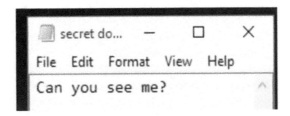

<u>Conclusion of the Book:</u>

You have reached the end of this text and I hope it has benefited you greatly. In the writing of this book, it was my desire to impart knowledge and methods which readers could use to increase their understanding of computer technology. In addition, many sections are directly dedicated to both building computer as well as gaining computer technology-related certifications. I hope you have benefited from my work and I wish you great success in all your adventures in computer technology. Remember, "Knowledge First in All Matters!!!!"

CPSIA information can be obtained
at www.ICGtesting.com
Printed in the USA
LVHW051953030820
662268LV00011B/747

9 781798 860151